WHO GOES BARE?

by

RICHARD HARRIS

and

LESLIE DARBON

SAMUEL   FRENCH

LONDON

NEW YORK   TORONTO   SYDNEY   HOLLYWOOD

CHARACTERS

Edward Manchip
Brian Manchip
Joan Manchip
Nancy McSmith
Angus McSmith
Maxie Maudlin
Minnie
Mrs Court-Bending
Mr Butcher
Police Sergeant

The action passes in the entrance hall to a country mansion

ACT I
  Scene 1   A late afternoon in autumn
  Scene 2   A few minutes later

ACT II   A few minutes later

Time – the present

ACT I

SCENE 1

The large entrance hall to a country mansion. A late afternoon in autumn

On one side a staircase leads to a gallery off which open four doors, each to a bedroom, numbered 1, 2, 3, and 4. An archway leads off to another stair-case which is not visible. Below the stairs is a swing door marked Staff Rooms, and opposite this is the main entrance to the hallway. At the rear of the hall, beneath the gallery, are three more doors. The centre one is a swing door marked Treatment Rooms; on one side is a sliding door to a cupboard; on the other a swing door marked Gymnasium. There is a reception desk with a telephone, a service bell and a jug of water. There are various occasional chairs and three antiquated heating radiators. Next to the Staff Room is a wall telephone. A large banner poster proclaims "Healthy is Happy" and there are several other posters, including one suggesting that "Abstinence Can Be Fun". Above the lower landing of the stairs is a large stained-glass window. The double casement opens outwards on to a rural view. Next to the window is a bentwood hatstand bearing a couple of men's hats. The general feeling of the place is that of a rich man's folly which in its time has played many parts. There is an air of seediness: funds would appear to be limited

When the CURTAIN *rises, the stage is empty. Then Mr Butcher enters through the main doors. He is carrying Eddie over his shoulder. Eddie's down-stretched hand clutches a bottle of vodka. Eddie Manchip is a tall, usually elegant, dilettante ladies' man of somewhat unctuous charm. Conscious of being forty, he favours clothing at least fifteen years too young for him. At the moment, his suit is crumpled, his tie awry, a gay handkerchief dangles from his top pocket. He looks terrible: the product of a lost week-end. Mr Butcher is a huge, square man in a huge, dark square suit and black hat. He pauses just inside the door, looking around, then moves to lower Eddie into the chair by the desk*

Mr Butcher (*shaking his shoulder*) Wakey wakey, my old china.
Eddie (*dazed*) Where am I?
Mr Butcher 'Ome. I've brought you 'ome. Now *there's* service for you.
Eddie (*getting shakily to his feet*) Thank you, my good man. (*He pats his pockets*) I don't seem to have my . . .
Mr Butcher No, no, Eddie. No need for *that*.

Eddie gives a weak smile and slumps into the chair again, clutching his aching head. Mr Butcher surveys the place

Mr Butcher Nice little place you've got here, Eddie. The boys *will* be
pleased.

Eddie Boys?

Mr Butcher Butcher, they said, take our friend Eddie the Elf back to his
house in the country.

Eddie Butcher?

Mr Butcher Don't tell me you've forgotten your new *friends*.

Eddie I know this sounds ridiculous, Mr Butcher—but could you refresh
my memory a little?

Mr Butcher The *card* game. At the *club*.

Eddie Oh. (*Realizing*) Oh.

Mr Butcher Eddie the Elf—none of the firm could work it out—why does
he call himself Eddie the Elf we arsked ourselves—but now I understand
—it's because you run an *Elf* Club.

Eddie Yes, it all falls into place, doesn't it? (*He stands shakily*) I expect
you're anxious to dash off home and explain it to them.

Mr Butcher Hang about, Eddie . . . hang about. There's still the question
of *this*.

He produces a piece of paper. Eddie moves to take it

Uh-uh—naughty, naughty.

Eddie Yes, of course. What exactly *is* it?

Mr Butcher Your I O U. From the card game.

Eddie You don't mean . . . ?

Mr Butcher So if we can just square up.

Eddie What exactly *do* I O U?

Mr Butcher (*reading*) I O U the deeds of my property. So if you'll just
hand them over . . .

Eddie Certainly. (*Realizing*) You mean *this* place?

Mr Butcher That's *exactly* what I mean.

Eddie That's impossible.

Butcher Nothing's impossible if you try, Eddie boy.

Eddie But I was blind drunk.

Mr Butcher (*holding out his hand*) The deeds.

Eddie Just as a matter of interest—what would happen if I refused?

Mr Butcher Well now—the organization would move in and redecorate
the place.

Eddie How nice.

Mr Butcher Blood red.

Eddie (*staggering a little*) My favourite colour.

Mr Butcher Ours, too. On the other hand, there's an alternative.

Eddie I'm all ears.

Mr Butcher For the time being. Shall we say—twenty thousand?

Eddie Twenty thousand *pounds*?

Butcher You *are* quick.

Eddie Where can I get my hands on twenty thousand pounds?

Mr Butcher You seem to get them on everything else, you naughty man,
you. Which reminds me—Loretta said to remind you, you've got a

little something of hers. Well then, Eddie boy—it's the house or twenty thousand—*you* think about it while I have a little walk. (*Moving to the main doors*) Incidentally—you don't know of a gravel pit near here, do you?

Eddie No.

Mr Butcher Pity. The boys'll have to bring their shovels. And it's bound to be clay.

Mr Butcher gives a flat smile and exits

Eddie, paralysed with fear, shakily pours himself a vodka

Minnie enters from the Staff Rooms. She is very short and lumpy, and wears thick pebble glasses for short sight. She is dressed in a white mob-cap, white overalls and white plimsolls. In her top pocket is a row of pens and pencils. Sticking out from another pocket is a yellow duster

Minnie Oh—there you are, Mister Edward, sir: welcome home.

Eddie Minnie—what *day* is it?

Minnie Saturday, sir.

Eddie *Saturday?* (*He winces at his head movement*)

Minnie It was when I woke up this morning, sir. Can I get you something for your head?

Eddie Yes—a transplant. On second thoughts, just an aspirin.

Minnie Yes, sir.

She finds the aspirins in her pocket, pops them into his mouth. He swallows them down with a glass of vodka

Good do, was it, sir?

Eddie Do?

Minnie The Health Conference.

Eddie Health Conference? Yes, of course—the *Health* Conference. Refresh my memory, Minnie: when did it start?

Minnie On Thursday, sir.

Eddie It seems to have gone on a bit. (*He pulls out the pocket handkerchief which he reveals to be a pair of panties. Playing cards flutter from his pocket also. Referring to the panties*) In fact it seems to have gone on a bit more than I thought. (*He stuffs the panties back into his pocket*)

Minnie (*picking up the cards*) You've not been gambling again, sir?

Eddie No, no, no—of course not, Minnie: I must have been playing patience. In between sessions.

Minnie Only I know what you're like once you enter the Metropolis.

Eddie (*suddenly very fearful*) What have I *done*, Minnie?

Minnie It'll all come back to you, sir.

Eddie It already *has*—and it's *enormous*.

Minnie Well, if you're going to do it, you might as well do it big, I always say. By the way, your brother telephoned, sir.

Eddie My brother? What did *he* want?

✴ TAXI

4 Who Goes Bare?

Minnie He said—(*she closes her eyes in concentration*)—my E.T.A. is fifteen-twenty hours, traffic and weather conditions permitting. Over and out.

Eddie E.T.A.? Why can't he just say he'll be arriving here at—(*realizing, looking at his watch*)—three-*twenty*. Oh, my god—you didn't tell him where I was?

Minnie Yes, sir—I said you were at the Health Conference.

Eddie That's right—yes—of course I was. Now look—Minnie. My brother is coming down here for the week-end with a very important visitor. A lady. A lady who is going to invest money in this place. She could be the answer to all our problems . . .

Minnie Oh, sir—oh, sir . . .

Eddie It's imperative that everyone's on their toes. Go and call the rest of the staff.

Minnie Yes, sir—yes, sir—no, sir—no. I forgot to tell you, sir . . .

Eddie Tell me *what*?

✴ *A car horn sounds. He looks towards the main doors, then bundles her towards the Staff Rooms*

All right, Minnie—leave it to me.

Minnie But, sir . . .

Eddie No buts, Minnie—off you go . . .

Eddie gets Minnie into the Staff Rooms as Brian Manchip enters from the main doors. In his early forties, shorter, tubbier, stodgier, than his brother. In fact a pompous prig. Although it's the week-end, he wears black jacket and striped trousers, beautifully polished black shoes. As he enters, he is tetchily dusting his hands over his jacket

Brian Edward! Ah—there you are.

Eddie Hello, Brian old son—good drive down?

Brian Appalling. Close the window and you suffocate—open it and you choke. Look at the state I'm in—look at me—filthy. (*He takes the panties from Eddie's pocket, sees what they are*) What were *these* doing in your top pocket?

Eddie Those? Those are a pocket handkerchief.

Brian I see. *These* is a pocket handkerchief.

Eddie Of course they is.

Brian *Are* it, indeed.

Eddie A novelty pocket handkerchief.

Brian Looking exactly like a pair of knickers.

Eddie Of course. That's the novelty. (*He retrieves the panties, stuffs them into his pocket*) The—er—the little lady with you, is she?

Brian If by "little lady" you mean Nancy McSmith—no, she is not. She's coming by train.

Eddie (*knowingly*) Of course.

Brian Now look here, Edward: I'm a highly respected man—both in my private and my business affairs. Everything I've done has been above board——

Eddie —until now.

Brian Are you trying to suggest . . .

Eddie Not *me*. But you know how some people's minds work. A man takes someone else's wife away for the week-end—let's face it—you could be up to *anything*.

Brian Ridiculous!

Eddie In *your* case, absolutely.

Brian On the other hand——

Eddie } —discretion. { *Speaking*
Brian }   { *together*

Eddie Naturally.

Brian Yes—well . . . (*He looks at his watch*) Nancy McSmith's train is due in half an hour—now—which room is she having?

Eddie Number One—best in the house.

Brian goes up to peer into Room 1. As he does so, Eddie—worry showing— moves to look out of the main doors

Brian Yes, that's all right. Which is my room?

Eddie Number Two.

Brian puts his head briefly into Room 2, considers it in juxtaposition to Room 1, then moves along to look into Room 4

Brian I think I'd prefer *this* one. (*He comes downstairs, indicating the place*) Look at the place. Look at it. Why did I ever let you trick me into putting up the money for this—this *mausoleum*?

Eddie Health Club, if you don't mind.

Brian Let me warn you, Edward: this is your last chance. If anything goes wrong this week-end—*finished*.

Eddie My dear Brian—what could possibly go wrong—with you at the wheel?

Brian (*after thinking a moment*) Yes—well—I told her I come here at least twice a week—I must know every *inch* of the place—what's in here?

Without waiting, he bustles out through the Treatment Rooms door. Eddie almost goes to the main doors but changes his mind and exits quickly after Brian. Minnie sticks her head round the Staff Room door. She enters and moves to the store cupboard. She is about to open the door when Eddie enters quickly from the Treatment Rooms

Eddie Minnie. Where is the staff?

Minnie That's what I was trying to tell you, sir. They've gone.

Eddie Gone?

Minnie Yes, sir. They had a meeting to express their discontent re the financial situation and—hopped it.

Eddie *All* of them?

Minnie *Not me*, sir—*not me* . . .

Eddie What about Gladys?

Minnie Him, too, sir. He had this incredible proposition on the Kings Road.

Eddie Why didn't they tell me.

Minnie They voted me spokesman, sir—on account of our peculiar relationship.

Eddie How could they do it to me? *Me*. After all I've—didn't I give them a bonus at Christmas?

Minnie They were all very pleased, sir, I know they were.

Eddie Then what's their complaint?

Minnie I think it's because they didn't get anything for the rest of the year.

Eddie Details, Minnie, details. What have they done to me?

Minnie A martyr: that's what you are, sir—a martyr.

Brian (*off, calling*) Edward!

Eddie Whatever you do, Minnie, say *nothing*.

Minnie What about?

Eddie *Anything.*

Brian enters from the Treatment Rooms.

On seeing him, Minnie does her curtsying and dusting bit

Brian Where on earth is the *staff*?

Eddie Around, old son, *around*.

Brian I haven't seen a *soul* yet.

Eddie Really? Well, *there's* one for a start.

He indicates Minnie who is now dusting maniacally. Brian stands open-mouthed as Minnie curtsies and dusts her way out backwards into the Staff Rooms

Minnie exits

Brian Why does she keep jigging up and down all the time? (*He vaguely imitates Minnie's curtsies*)

Eddie She's a born servant.

Brian What exactly does she *do* here?

Eddie Anything I ask. She came with the place. I think one of the builders must have left her. She's in love with me. On the rebound. She was jilted by a pirate.

Brian A pirate?

Eddie We had a fancy dress ball—someone came as a pirate and Minnie fell in love with him.

Brian You mean she doesn't know who he was?

Eddie He swore a promise of eternal love and disappeared.

Brian I'm not surprised.

Eddie Tragic really: she's been mooning over him ever since.

Brian Which reminds me—Nancy McSmith is the wife of one of my most valued business clients. *Don't try your luck.*

Eddie My dear Brian. To me, she's just a cheque-book with a human appendage.

Brian Well, keep your hands off her counterfoils. (*He looks at his watch*) I must go. (*Moving to the main doors*) If my wife telephones, I haven't arrived yet. And whatever you do don't mention Nancy.

Eddie You mean Joan doesn't know you're bringing her here?

Brian (*shocked*) Are you *mad*?

Eddie Don't tell me she's still jealous?

Brian Jealous? She'd be jealous if I was run over by a woman *driver*.

Eddie Jealous of you? I mean, it really is ridiculous.

Brian (*haughtily*) What are you trying to say?

Eddie Well, let's face it—if you were marooned on a desert island with Raquel Welch, you'd use her to build a raft.

Brian Nonsense. (*Pause*) Who *is* Raquel Welch?

Eddie grimaces

I'm talking about my wife.

Eddie Your wife. Now there's reality for you. What does she think you're *doing* here?

Brian Actually I was rather firm. I told her I was very ill. Sick. I've come down here for a rest. You see what I've done for you? Lied—to my own wife.

Eddie I know: It's almost human.

Brian So if she does telephone, I can't speak to her because I'm in bed, pulling myself together.

Eddie With Nancy McSmith . . .

Brian Will you please stop . . .

Eddie You misunderstand me. What I mean is, you *can't* be in bed doing your own little thing because as far as Nancy McSmith is concerned, you're a bundle of health.

Brian Am I?

Eddie Of course you are: you told her you come here twice a week. The whole point is for you to *impress* her.

Brian You're absolutely right. (*Pause*) How do I do it?

Eddie With your *body*. It's got to be bouncing with health and vitality. Like those budgerigars you see on television.

Brian Do they *really* bounce?

Eddie Certainly: and they're only actors. You're the real thing. Well— almost.

Brian (*suddenly worried*) There's nothing that can go wrong, is there?

Eddie Nothing in the world.

Brian I mean—there's nothing I should know about? (*He puts a brotherly arm round Eddie*)

Eddie Brian old son—if anything *had* happened, you'd be the last to know about it.

Brian isn't quite sure how to take this

Brian Then let me warn you, Edward: my present financial situation is extremely precarious.

Eddie Where's all this money *gone* then?

Brian Frankly, I've frittered it all away on income tax. So remember, Edward—let me down—and it will be the end—for *both* of us. (*He glares at Eddie and moves to the main doors*) I must meet that train. And for God's sake get this place looking healthy!

Brian exits by the main doors. Minnie enters from the Staff Rooms

Eddie Minnie.

Minnie Yes, sir?

Eddie For God's sake get this place looking healthy!

Minnie Yes, sir—yes, sir . . . (*She looks around, then crosses to open the window. She whips out her duster to wave in some air*)

Meanwhile, Eddie goes to the poster and pours himself another vodka

Eddie What's the point, Minnie? What am I going to do? Apart from anything else, I'm dead skint.

Minnie (*shyly*) I want you to know, sir—that if ever you need anything financial—like money—you have only to ask.

Eddie I know that, Minnie.

Minnie Truly, sir: everything I have is yours for the taking.

Eddie (*snapping out of it*) I can't lose this opportunity—this place is like a millstone round my neck—I've got to impress this Nancy McSmith *somehow*—but how can I do it when there's no-one here to *do* it with? No clients—no staff—if nothing else, I've got to have *staff* . . .

Minnie There's *me*, sir—there's always *me*.

Eddie But I need expert staff—therapists—hairdressers—masseuses . . .

Minnie (*in ecstasy*) Masseuses! Oh, sir—oh, sir—if only you knew how I've lived for this moment . . . (*She dashes over to the cupboard and pulls out the wheelchair to swing it round. Sitting in the chair is what appears to be an old man swathed in blankets with a suitcase on his lap*)

Eddie can only stare as Minnie takes the suitcase and puts it on the floor to open it. She kneels to pull out a doctor's stethoscope, a hammer, a huge bottle of horse embrocation, a paperback book, huge scissors

If only you knew how I've studied on your behalf—for years I've crimped and shaved—for years I've studied books in the most pertinent detail. (*She holds up a book*) Do It Yourself Massage—and very hard it was too, sir—you name it, I've massaged it. (*She gets to her feet to snatch the blankets from the figure to reveal that it is a life-size sorbo dummy—naked. She throws the dummy face-down on the floor and starts to "massage" it feverishly*) Look, sir—look.

Eddie (*dazed*) I can't *believe* it.

Minnie It's true, sir—it's *me*—your Minnie.

Eddie (*standing up and snapping out of his horror*) Get that thing out of here! You'll frighten people to death! (*Desperately, again*) *What* people? Get rid of it—burn it!

Minnie clings protectively to the dummy

Minnie I couldn't, sir—not my Phillip—not my prince—I beg you, spare his life. Without him I am nothing. (*She is on the point of another break-down*)
Eddie All right, all right. Just keep it out of the way—*please*—and get this stuff out of here.

Minnie gets on hands and knees and begins collecting her equipment and bunging it into the suitcase. Eddie paces, then comes to a decision

There isn't time to get anyone else. You'll have to help me.
Minnie Oh, sir!
Eddie But I beg you, Minnie—don't use your initiative—do only what I tell you to do.
Minnie I will, sir—I will . . .
Eddie I don't want to see you hanging around, Minnie. (*He moves closer to Minnie*) You've got to distribute yourself—somehow you've got to make yourself look like a highly qualified team of experts. I don't know how, but we'll do it.
Minnie Oh, I will, sir—I will . . .
Eddie (*moving to the stairs*) And get that thing out of here.

Eddie exits to the Staff Rooms

Minnie is in raptures. She jerks the dummy upright and kisses it

Minnie Oh, Phillip—Phillip—it's like a dream come true. Don't think I don't appreciate your muscles—but I've always wanted to get my hands on a real one, and now . . .
Mrs Court-Bending (*off*) Hello there!

At the sound of the voice Minnie gets the dummy and wheelchair back into the cupboard, closes the cupboard door, and turns

Mrs Court-Bending enters. A hale, middle-aged county lady

Hello there—Mr Manchip about—is he?
Minnie I'll find him for you, madam.
Mrs Court-Bending Not to worry—can't stop—just popped in to remind him about the jolly old jumble. He didn't mention it, I suppose?
Minnie Not within earshot, no, madam.
Mrs Court-Bending Briefly put you in the picture—the name's Court-Bending—spoke to him on the blower couple've days ago—collecting old clothes for Oxfam—said he'd sort something out—obviously hasn't —jolly good cause—doing me best—here, have a brochure. (*She takes*

out a piece of paper and gives it to Minnie, then looks at her watch) **Pop** back later then—don't forget—tell him I called.

Minnie is peering short-sightedly at the brochure. She looks up and curtsies

Minnie From Oxford. Yes, madam, I'll tell him.
Mrs Court-Bending Jolly good. Cheer-oh!

Mrs Court-Bending exits

Minnie curtsies, then stares at the brochure again

Minnie *(reading)* Oxford Famine Relief! Oxford. Well I never . . . all them poor students . . .

Minnie exits, still reading, to the Treatment Rooms.
    Eddie, in a change of clothing, enters from the Staff Rooms. As he reaches the foot of the stairs Brian enters urgently through the main doors

Brian Edward—she's here.
Eddie There's something I ought to tell you . . .
Brian Later—later . . .

Nancy enters. She's a strapping woman in her twenties. She wears the mini-est of clothing and carries only a small vanity case

Nancy *(with a smile)* Hello.
Eddie *(impressed)* Hello.
Brian Nancy—I want you to meet my brother, Edward. Edward—let me introduce a wonderful lady, Nancy McSmith—*(pointedly)*—Mrs *Angus* McSmith.
Eddie I don't think I've had the pleasure.
Brian That makes a change. Incidentally—what did you tell your husband?
Nancy Angus? I said I was spending the week-end with my mother.
Brian Oh.
Nancy He just doesn't understand about places like this.
Brian Where *is* he?
Nancy He's away for the week-end—adjudicating at a porridge festival.
Brian I never knew he did that sort of thing.
Nancy Oh, yes—he's always been a great one for his oats.
Eddie I'll fetch your luggage.

Nancy hands him the vanity case. Eddie looks from the case to Brian

Nancy Do show me to my room—I'm dying to get out of these clothes.
Eddie You almost are. *(He pointedly takes the case from Nancy) I'll* show you up. *(He guides Nancy towards the stairs)* It's room number one—the best in the house.

Nancy, on the landing, looks out of the window

Nancy Oh, look—a swimming pool—shall we go and see?
Brian Us? Oh, yes—lovely.

Nancy, moving back down the stairs, indicates the Staff Rooms door

Nancy This way?
Eddie (*indicates*) Straight through.

Nancy exits

Nancy (*as she goes*) I'm so looking forward to this week-end.
Brian (*an obvious lie*) Me, too.

Brian exits after her

(*As he goes, with a hiss at Eddie*) Why is it so cold in here?

Eddie watches his exit with relief

Minnie enters from the Treatment Rooms

Eddie Minnie—why is it so cold in here?
Minnie It's the heating, sir.
Eddie I know it's the heating. Why isn't it?
Minnie Why isn't it what, sir?
Eddie The boiler—why isn't it heating?
Minnie Its been off it's food for days, sir. I bung coal in and it just lies there—staring at me.
Eddie First the staff leaves now the boiler goes out. I'll have a look at it.
Minnie It would like that, sir—I know it would.

Eddie almost exits to the Treatment Rooms but pauses

Eddie Minnie—don't forget—the lady is very important—you've got to give her the full treatment. She is our salvation.
Minnie Oh, I will, sir—I will . . .

Eddie looks at her hopelessly and exits to the Treatment Rooms

Minnie is about to exit to the Staff Rooms when we hear the sound of a car horn. She freezes, then dashes across to look out through the main doors

A taxi. It's her—I've got to give her the full treatment! (*She looks around wildly then whips out a duster and starts dusting the cupboard door*)

Joan enters carrying a suitcase identical to Minnie's. She is an attractive woman in her thirties, fashionably dressed. She looks at the dusting Minnie and puts down the suitcase

Minnie curtsies across to the desk and sits

Minnie (*in a receptionist voice*) You rang, madam?
Joan I'd like to see my husband.
Minnie Oh, yes?
Joan Mr Manchip.
Minnie You've made a mistake, madam. Mr Manchip isn't married.
Joan I'm talking about his brother.
Minnie I can assure you, madam, that if Mr Manchip had married his
    brother, *I* would have been one of the first to know. I'd go so far as to
    say I would have been a bridesmaid.
Joan I am Mr Edward's sister-in-law. That is, I married his brother,
    Brian. And I want to see him.
Minnie Yes, of course you do, madam. But first things first. Have you
    been here before?
Joan I've always managed to avoid it.
Minnie I'll have to make out a form then.
Joan Is that necessary?
Minnie Oh, yes—they always make out a form.
Joan (*all patience gone*) Just what exactly do you want to know?

*Minnie stands up, produces a steel tape-measure and moves round to vaguely
hold it up against Joan, making notes*

Minnie We'll begin with height, weight and other physical peculiarities.
Joan Do you *always* treat people like this?
Minnie Oh, no, madam. But then you're special. You are our salvation.
    How long will you be staying?
Joan Just for the week-end, thank God.
Minnie I'll prepare your room. That is, I'll advise one of the several
    chambermaids of your proximity.

*Minnie curtsies—and backing away as though to royalty—goes up the
stairs into Room 1*

Joan I think *I* shall be the one with the nervous breakdown. (*She takes up
    the card Minnie has written on*) Height—average. Weight—average.
    Physical peculiarities—yes. Oh, charming. (*She tosses the card back on
    the desk and raps her fingers impatiently on the desk*) Where is everyone?

Joan exits to the Gymnasium

*Eddie enters from the Treatment Rooms, sees Joan's suitcase and moves
to take it up*

Eddie (*calling*) Minnie!

Minnie enters from Room 1 to wave a feather duster from the gallery

Minnie Yes, sir?

Eddie (*of the suitcase*) I told you to get rid of this.

Minnie Rid of what, sir?

Eddie *This.* Look—I'll put it in the store cupboard. Get rid of it as soon as you've finished doing whatever it is you're doing. (*He goes to toss the suitcase into the cupboard*)

Minnie exits to Room 1. Joan enters from the Gymnasium

Joan Edward.

Eddie (*turns, shocked*) Joan! That is—I mean—*Joan.* (*He kisses her*)

Joan I've come to spend the week-end with my husband.

Eddie But he's sick—*ill.*

Joan Precisely. And like the fool I am, I worry about him.

Eddie But that's why he's here—to get away from you—I mean—not *you* —*everyone.*

Joan A wife's place is by her husband's side. Especially when he's with someone like *you.*

Eddie Oh, my God. You still don't trust me.

Joan No I don't trust me. You're a bad influence.

Eddie I admit I have my weak moments.

Joan Unfortunately your *weak* moments last for *years.*

Eddie Unfair. Unfair.

Joan A fine reception this is, I must say.

Eddie If only you'd *said* you were coming.

Joan (*suspiciously*) Why are you so concerned?

Eddie Let's not talk about us—let's talk about Brian. The man is sick.

Joan Sick? He certainly is.

Eddie The thing is—he needs to be left alone.

Joan From what I can see, he's come to the right place.

Eddie Therefore—speaking not as his brother, but as his health adviser— notwithstanding how much you worry about him and want to look after him—I think you should go.

Joan I shall.

Eddie I knew you'd see sense.

Joan To my room. (*She moves to the stairs*)

Minnie comes stumbling out of Room 1 and down the stairs dusting as she comes, to curtsy

Minnie Lovely room that, madam. Goes with your hair.

Joan Thank you. Please tell my husband I'm here.

Joan exits to Room 1

Minnie takes off her glasses to dust them, showing how short-sighted she is. Eddie is lost in thought

Minnie I'll go and find him, sir.

Eddie Who?

Minnie Madam's husband.

Eddie He's in the garden. No! The thing is it's very important that he doesn't know his wife is here.

Minnie But madam *said*, sir . . .

Eddie Yes, I know that, Minnie—the thing is—it's his birthday.

Minnie Oh, I see, sir: you want it to be a surprise.

Eddie That's it, Minnie: probably the biggest surprise he's had in his life —so we'll only let him in on it when I've thought of something—that is, at the right moment. (*Fingers to lips*) Mum's the word.

Minnie puts her fingers to lips, enjoying the spirit of the occasion

Minnie (*whispering*) I'm sure the lady will be very happy in number one, sir.

Eddie (*whispering*) I'm sure she will. (*With a sudden thought, and back to his normal voice*) Number *one*? That room was for the *other* lady.

Minnie (*looking round*) What other lady?

Eddie The lady I told you was very important.

Minnie Oh, that one's a very important lady, sir. Treated me like a dog, she did.

Eddie Minnie—there's *another* lady coming—don't you remember?

Minnie Oh, that's right, sir—the lady from Oxford.

Eddie Oxford?

Minnie The Welfare lady with all those starving students.

Eddie What starving students?

Minnie All those starving students in Oxford, sir. Look, sir—I'll show you. (*She pulls out the crumpled brochure and hands it to Eddie*) Tragic it is, sir. They eat clothes.

Eddie Minnie—they don't *eat* the clothes, they *sell* them to buy food.

Minnie That's not what I was given to understand, sir.

Eddie Minnie—when the lady comes, we'll give her some clothes, I promise you. I want you to try and think about the *other* lady.

Minnie Oh, sir—don't tell me they're having a hard time in Cambridge . . .

Eddie The one who's with my brother!

Minnie Oh. A-*nother* lady!

Eddie *Yes*, Minnie. Now will you please go and prepare a room for her— number *three*. And remember—distribute yourself.

Minnie curtsies away and scuttles up the stairs and into Room 3. Joan enters from Room 1

Joan Where *is* he?

Eddie Just coming. (*He waves towards the main rooms*)

Joan Why is it so cold in my room?

Eddie Cold? (*He rubs his brow*) I'm feeling rather hot myself.

Joan Either *do* something—or I want another room.

Joan glares at him and exits to Room 1. Nancy and Brian enter from the Staff Rooms

Eddie (*weakly*) Back so soon?

Brian I was just telling Nancy how peaceful it is down here.

Eddie Ha! Peaceful! What? Incredibly.

Throughout the following he's very much aware of Joan in Room 1 and makes desperate signals to Brian who just doesn't understand. When Eddie points upstairs, Brian thinks he means the window

Brian Incidentally, who was that hanging about at the end of the drive?

Eddie What did he look like?

Brian mimes a large box

The Butcher?

Brian The Butcher.

Eddie Our—local butcher.

Brian What was he doing here?

Eddie He came to give me the chop—a chop.

Nancy I thought you'd be a vegetarian.

Eddie So I would be—if I didn't eat meat.

Nancy *I'm* supposed to be a vegetarian—but I must admit I do sometimes have a bit on the side.

Eddie How very interesting.

Nancy He seemed quite a character.

Eddie The Butcher? He is—yes, he is. Did you—er—did you speak to him?

Brian He seemed rather preoccupied—chopping down a tree.

Eddie How incredibly rustic.

Nancy With the side of his hand.

She mimes a karate chop. Eddie staggers a little

Minnie enters from Room 3 and comes down, curtsying

Minnie The room's all ready, sir—not for the lady with all those starving students—or for the lady what treats me like a dog—or would do if she was here which she isn't and we all like a nice surprise, don't we sir? No—the lady from Cambridge, sir.

Still curtsying, Minnie backs into the Treatment Rooms

Brian and Nancy look from her to Eddie

Eddie Sweet, isn't she?

Brian I'll show Nancy to her room. Room number one . . .

Eddie moves quickly to them and tries to relieve Brian of the vanity case. It becomes a struggle

Eddie Actually it's room number three.

Brian We agreed that number one was the best room . . .

Eddie Yes, of course, we did. Now it's room number three. (*He finally*

gets possession of the case. To Nancy) The room's the same, it's just that
every so often, we change the numbers on the doors. It's so easy to
get into a rut, don't you agree?
Nancy Oh, I do. That's why I came to a place like this. Somewhere where
one can feel *free*. (*She makes an expansive gesture of freedom*)
Brian Yes—well—Room number *free* then. (*He laughs feebly at his "joke"*)

Eddie guides Nancy upstairs, still trying to make warning signals to Brian

Eddie I'll show Nancy to her room. You fill out her form.
Brian Does it *need* filling out?
Eddie (*waving at desk*) The *form*. I can't understand it, he knows it's the
form to fill out the form.

Eddie opens the door to Room 3. Nancy leans in

Nancy Oh—what a wonderful view.
Eddie (*referring to her*) Wonderful—yes—wonderful.

*Eddie and Nancy exit to Room 3, Eddie making a final despairing signal at
Room 1*

Brian Form? What form? (*He moves to the desk*)
Joan (*off; calling*) Edward? What have you done with my husband?
Brian (*freezing*) My wife!

*Brian dashes into the cupboard, sliding the door shut as Joan enters.
Minnie enters from the Treatment Rooms as Joan comes downstairs*

Joan Have you seen my husband?
Minnie What does he look like, madam?
Joan He's short, round and very ill.
Minnie Oh, dear. He should see a doctor.
Joan Exactly what *I* said.
Minnie I thought *I* did.
Joan Yes, you did.
Minnie Did I?
Joan Yes.
Minnie And did he?
Joan Did he what?
Minnie See a doctor.
Joan No.
Minnie No wonder he's ill then.

Joan gives up and storms out through the Gymnasium door

*Now that the coast is clear, Minnie looks around, goes quickly to the cup-
board door. She opens it. We see that the dummy is standing upright. She
reaches in and pulls it out, revealing that it was being held there by Brian
who stands with his eyes firmly shut, expecting the worse. Minnie has taken
out the dummy without any acknowledgement of Brian. Now she shuts the*

door and starts to move away, stops, then moves back to open the cupboard door. Brian stands in exactly the same position as we last saw him

Minnie Oh. It's you, sir. I thought it was the bank manager.
Brian Oh really?
Minnie Might I wish you a Happy Birthday?
Brian Thank you, Minnie.

With no more ado, Minnie slides the door shut and carries the dummy into the Staff Rooms.
    Door 3 and Eddie comes out and hurries downstairs, as Brian enters fearfully from the cupboard

Brian (*pointing towards the bedroom*) Joan—she's here . . .
Eddie I know—I know. You've got to persuade her to leave.
Brian How can I? When have I ever been able to persuade her to do *anything*?
Eddie You'll think of something.
Brian *You* think of something.
Eddie I've already thought what to *do*—all you've got to do is *do* it. (*He hurries back upstairs*)
Brian Where are you going?
Eddie To keep Nancy in her room.

Eddie exits to Room 3. Brian looks around desperately, then exits quickly to the Gymnasium.
    Minnie enters from the Staff Rooms, singing Happy Birthday to You. She moves to the window, looks out, and exits to the Treatment Rooms. Brian, coughing, and Joan enter from the Gymnasium

Joan and Brian are in the middle of an argument. Note: *whenever Brian is with Joan he acts the "sick man"*

Joan I've no intention of returning to London. Now that I'm here, I'm here to stay.
Brian But you *can't stay.*
Joan Why not?
Brian Because—because I'm ill. (*He gives a little wheeze*)
Joan Which is precisely why I'm staying.
Brian But don't you understand? If you're here, I shall be worrying about you. I should be *resting*. (*He collapses into a chair, chest heaving dramatically*)
Joan (*suddenly*) Who is Nancy?

It is so sudden that Brian is pulled up with a jolt

Brian (*weakly*) Nancy?
Joan I just happened to be rubbing a pencil over your telephone pad when I distinctly made out the outline of today's date and the name Nancy.
Brian Oh—*that* Nancy.

Joan *Which* Nancy?

Brian Nancy—you know—(*quickly*)—The National Association of Nautical and Cinematographic Yachtsmen.

Joan The National Association of *what*?

Brian (*quickly*) Neurotics and Cricketing Yorkshiremen. It's their anniversary. I send them a donation. (*He coughs to remind her that he's ill and clasps at a sudden pain in his back*)

Joan You should be in bed.

Brian I know—I know . . .

Joan moves to him and kisses his forehead

Joan My poor darling—I'm so worried about you. (*She kisses him again*) It's just that I don't trust that brother of yours. If it's not one thing it's the other.

Brian I admit he's sometimes asked me for a bit of money, but he's never asked me for a bit of the other.

Joan (*pointing upstairs*) Come on. Bed.

Brian I think I'll just have a quick lie down in the sauna bath.

Brian hurries—then remembers, and limps—to exit to the Treatment Rooms

Joan climbs the stairs, closing the window as she goes

As Joan gets to the top, Eddie enters from Room 3, slamming the door, and clutches the door handle

Joan (*after looking at him for a moment*) Why are you hanging on to that door handle?

Eddie Am I? So I am. Yes. I'm testing it. (*He rattles the handle*) You see, if anyone was stuck inside, I could shake the handle and shout out: (*He shouts at the door*) It's all right! The door's stuck! I'll let you out in a minute! (*Turning to Joan*) But of course it *isn't* stuck, so I don't have to shout. (*He shouts at the door*) Don't do anything! Just sit there quietly! (*To Joan*) All I have to do is shake the handle. Simple really.

Joan looks at him, then goes into Room 1, closing the door. Immediately Eddie dashes downstairs as Brian enters from the Treatment Rooms

Brian Joan refuses to leave!

Eddie What did you tell her?

Brian I said I was sick.

Eddie Never mind about Joan—what did you tell *Nancy*?

Brian Why?

Eddie *Why?* (*He points wildly upstairs*) She thinks this place is a *nudist* colony!

At this moment the door to Room 3 opens and Nancy comes out. She is "naked", covered by her long blonde hair and two tennis racquets

Eddie and Brian can only stare at her

Nancy Anyone for tennis?

The Lights fade to a quick Black-Out, as—

the CURTAIN *falls*

SCENE 2

A few minutes later

When the CURTAIN *rises, Eddie is discovered looking out of the open window Brian is pacing nervously*

Brian What's she doing?

Eddie Gambolling.

Brian Who with?

Eddie On the lawn. *Gambolling*. Up and down jumping. *Starkers*.

Brian (*despairingly*) What can we do?

Eddie Fetch the binoculars.

Brian Stop staring out of that window and *think*.

Eddie (*with an evil grin*) I *am* thinking. (*Concerned*) Anyway, it's your fault. What did you tell her about this place?

Brian I don't know. I can't understand it. All I said was that this is the Healthy Vale Sun Club.

Eddie No, no, no—The Sunny Vale *Health* Club!

Brian Is there a difference?

Eddie My dear Brian—when you go to a health club you take off weight. When you go to a sun club, you take off *everything*.

Brian Everything?

Eddie *Everything*. Witness gambolling Godiva out there.

Brian What sort of man does she think I am?

Eddie I dread to think.

Brian Now look here . . . (*Suddenly realizing*) Oh my God. (*He starts to climb the stairs*)

Eddie Where are you going?

Brian My wife. I've got to stop her looking out of the window.

Eddie (*pointing to the window*) You're supposed to be with the delectable Mrs McSmith . . .

Brian Will you stop trying to imply that there is anything going on between that dear lady——

Eddie —dear naked lady——

Brian —dear naked lady and myself . . . (*Suddenly remembering Nancy is outside*) Oh my god. (*He looks through the window and winces at what he sees*) Look at her. (*Imploring, to Nancy*) Keep *still*, madam. (*To God, hands in prayer*) I've never asked you for much—but couldn't you send

down just a *little* fog? (*To Eddie*) It's all a terrible mistake—but you're
right. Joan will never understand.

Eddie Right. *I'll* look after Joan—*you* look after Nancy.

Brian Yes. (*He moves to the Staff doors*)

Eddie Before you go . . .

Brian turns

Take your clothes off.

Brian Yes, of course. (*He starts to unbuttom his jacket, but realizes*) No,
I will not take my clothes off.

Eddie Look—*someone* has to convince Nancy that this is a nudist colony.

Brian Why?

Eddie Why? Because—one—we need the money—more than you know
—and two—if *she* finds out that you lied to her and tells her husband—
your most valued client—things could be very nasty—very nasty.

Brian I didn't lie to her. She misunderstood.

Eddie I see. Like Joan misunderstood.

Brian All right, all right. But she's got to find out sooner or later that
she's made a mistake.

Eddie Whatever happens, we've got to get that money out of her. So:
she wants to think this is a nudist colony. Which means seeing someone
else in the same state.

Brian Do you really expect me to go out there and—*frolic naked*?

Eddie No, no, no—it doesn't mean that you have to *appear* naked.

Brian No?

Eddie No. It means that you have to *appear* to appear naked.

Brian You mean . . . ?

Eddie *Of course.* You surely couldn't have thought that I meant . . .

Brian No, no. Of course not. I apologize.

Eddie I accept your apology. Off you go then.

*Eddie points upstairs. Brian moves to the stairs, looks out of the window at
Nancy then*

Brian Where to?

Eddie Your room.

Brian My room. Yes, of course. (*He takes a few more steps, then stops*)
Why?

Eddie So that when you reappear, you will appear to appear naked—
which is what we agreed.

Brian Did we?

Eddie Yes.

Brian So we did. (*He moves a few more steps up*) We did not!

Eddie Shall we discuss it with your wife?

Brian That's blackmail!

Eddie Isn't it!

*Brian fumes a moment, then hurries upstairs, clasps his hands to his head,
and exits to Room 4*

*As soon as Brian has gone, Eddie goes to swivel the poster and pour himself
a large vodka, and starts to drink*

   *Maxie Maudlin enters through the main doors. He is fifty, wears a check
   suit and fedora. He looks very twitchy, is grabbing at a bottle of pills*

Eddie is clearly amazed to see him

Maxie Eddie—Eddie . . .
Eddie *Maxie*—what do *you* want?
Maxie Water—water—a glass of water . . . (*He makes to take the glass
   from Eddie*)
Eddie That's neat vodka. (*He points to the desk*) Here—here—on the desk.

*Maxie goes to the desk, pours himself water from the jug and drinks down
some pills. He takes a deep breath, hand on heart*

Maxie You've got to help me, Eddie.
Eddie Help *you*—ha!
Maxie Tell me who I am.
Eddie Who you are?
Maxie Who am I?
Eddie You're Maxie Maudlin—the famous quick-change artist—The Man
   With a Thousand Faces . . .
Maxie That's just it, Eddie—I've got to have a rest—doctor's orders—
   they're taking me over.
Eddie Who are?
Maxie My masterful impersonations. I don't know who I *am* any more.
Eddie You mean like . . . ?
Maxie Exactly. Doctor Jekyll and Mister Maudlin—it's getting me down,
   Eddie—my life isn't my own any more—I can't stand it. It's getting
   worse! (*He grips Eddie's arm*) Eddie—you've got to let me have a room
   —just for a few days.
Eddie I can't have this place cluttered up with invalids—it's supposed to
   be a *health* club.
Maxie I beg of you, Eddie—I've got to find myself before it's too late . . .
Eddie I'd like to, Maxie, but—(*a sudden thought*)—hold on a minute.
   Have you got your costumes with you?
Maxie Me trunk's outside. I've come straight from a barmitzvah in the
   Balls Pond Road.

Suddenly Eddie is all charm: his arm goes round Maxie

Eddie Maxie—my dear old friend—you couldn't have come at a better time
   —*of course* you can have a room—*of course* you can stay here. For as
   long as you like. As my guest.
Maxie (*suspiciously*) There must be a catch.
Eddie It's like this, Maxie. The staff has hopped it. I need to convince a
   certain lady that they're still here—and highly efficient. You're the only
   one who can do it for me.

Maxie Me? How?

Eddie Simply by creating a few of your masterful impersonations.

Maxie (*apalled*) Not that, Eddie—I beg you—anything but that!

Eddie Nonsense, old son: after all I've done for *you*? All you've got to do is keep your eyes and ears open and put in an appearance as and when it becomes necessary. (*He rings the desk bell*) You can have Room Number Two—Minnie will bring your things up.

Maxie (*horrified*) *Minnie*—I thought she'd have been put down by now. I'm off.

He makes to go but Eddie restrains him

Eddie You can't go now.

Maxie Watch me.

Eddie I'll tell Minnie who her amorous pirate was.

Maxie I was drunk. . . . I had a black-out.

Eddie You must have done.

Minnie lurches in from the Treatment Rooms

Minnie (*curtsying*) You rang, sir?

Maxie presses himself back, trying to hide. He squeezes his eyes shut

Eddie Minnie, we have another guest—would you bring in his luggage, please—and take it straight up to room two.

Minnie Yes, sir—yes, sir . . .

Minnie curtsies towards the main doors, sees the shut-eyed Maxie, waggles her duster over him and exits

Maxie (*opening his eyes, amazed*) She didn't recognize me!

Eddie *Of course* she didn't—it's the *pirate* who fills her dreams. You're perfectly safe. (*A thought*) In fact, you're probably the only one who *is*.

Maxie If she finds out—think of it—sailing the seven seas with *her* on my back—doomed—like the Flying Dustman.

Eddie She won't find out—as long as you help me.

Maxie That's blackmail!

Eddie I know: it's the current craze. So it's either help *me*—or it's over the waves with that bow-legged Pandora out there.

Minnie crashes through the main doors with a huge trunk. The trunk is covered in seaside stickers. She staggers around under the weight of the trunk, staggers to the rear, watched by the frozen Maxie and Eddie, then lurches forward, almost falls into the pit, is saved by Maxie. She continues to weave precariously and finally finds the stairs. She gets a few steps up, then begins to descend backwards, Maxie and Eddie rush to her and succeed in giving her sufficient momentum to mount the stairs. They watch as she crashes into Room 2. There is an enormous crash. Then Minnie reappears minus the trunk, comes downstairs, curtsies and exits to the Staff Rooms

Eddie and Maxie have watched all this in silent horror. Now Eddie puts an arm round Maxie and guides him upstairs

Eddie The thing is, old son, I've got a terrible problem. The staff's all gone and we've got someone very important staying here this weekend . . .

We lose the words as they mount the stairs and move along the gallery, but still see Eddie explaining

Maxie (*as they reach Room 2; loudly*) You mean she's out there—*frolicing naked?*

Eddie Believe me—it's a matter of life and death . . .

Eddie ushers Maxie to Room 2, then moves along to Room 4, just as Brian puts his head out. He is holding his clothes

Ready?

Brian (*raising his eyes to heaven*) If there is a—you know—Someone Up There—he'll understand, won't he? He'll understand . . . ?

Eddie takes the pile from him, moving away

Eddie You might know the answer sooner than you think if you don't hurry up.

Brian What are you doing with my clothes?

Eddie Just making sure you play the game, old son. (*He hurries downstairs and tosses the clothes into the cupboard. He takes up his glass of vodka from the desk, and has a sip*

Brian comes out of his room. He is naked, apart from shoes and socks, but clutches a framed oil painting to cover his dignity. Slowly he comes downstairs

Eddie (*referring to the painting*) The Stag At Bay. Very appropriate.

Brian (*terrified*) What happens now?

Eddie You go into the garden and you gambol!

Brian I can't—I can't . . . !

Eddie Of course you can. (*Referring to his drink*) Bottoms up!

Nancy (*off*) Coo-eeee!

They freeze

Nancy appears at the window. We see enough of her to gather that she is naked. She waves a tennis racquet

Anyone for tennis?

Eddie Yes—Brian.

Brian No! That is—no-one *else* playing?

Nancy I was hoping for a mixed doubles but I can't find anyone.

Eddie They're all on the run. That's it—a cross-country run. Incredibly healthy. They'll be hours. Probably the rest of the day.

Nancy Oh well—*we'll* have a nice little game then, Brian.

Brain Us? Oh—yes—lovely. (*He mimes a tennis stroke and nearly dislodges the painting*)

Nancy Come on then—I'm dying to play with you.

Brian I think I've left the gas on—I mean, light on—in my room. You go and—get the net warmed up. With you in two shakes of a—that is, two minutes. (*He backs away up the stairs, out of her vision*)

Eddie That's it, Nancy—you toddle off and practise a few strokes—careful on the old backhand, eh?

Nancy See you later then.

Nancy skips off

Brian breathes a sigh of relief and comes downstairs. Eddie pours himself another vodka

Brian I can't play tennis like *this*. (*With a sudden thought*) I can't play *tennis*.

Eddie You'll have to.

Brian (*referring to the painting*) What about this?

Eddie Tell her you can't find your racquet.

Brian looks out of the window. He starts to bob up and down, obviously "accompanying" Nancy outside

Joan enters from Room 1

Eddie quickly puts his glass down near the water jug

Joan Brian!

Brian reacts in horror, keeps his back to her

Brian You recognized me!

Joan Where are your clothes?

Brian I—I . . .

Eddie As soon as he knew you were here, he dropped *everything*.

Brian moves to Eddie's side as though for protection

Joan (*coming downstairs*) How dare you let him walk about like that when he's so ill?

Unseen by Joan, Nancy appears at the window and tosses in a tennis ball, then exits

Brian instinctively catches the ball, Eddie catches the painting in front of Brian. Brian looks down at the painting, realizes what he did, and nearly faints. Eddie takes the ball and tosses it back through the window

Eddie Those damned woodpeckers! (*To Brian*) Off you go then, old chap—mustn't keep the lady waiting, must we?

Joan *What* lady?

Eddie The lady—that is, the *old* lady—the old *fat* lady—who's waiting to give him his massage. (*He ushers the unwilling Brian towards the Staff Rooms*)

Joan In the *garden*?

Eddie In the garden. Yes. Well. That's why he was standing there with no clothes on. (*To Brian*) Wasn't it?

Brian Yes.

Joan What was?

Eddie Yes.

Joan What was?

Eddie Yes. He was just on his way to the treatment rooms when he happened to notice this old painting.

Eddie taps the canvas. Brian winces

Joan What about the painting.

Eddie Yes—what *about* it?

Brian He asked me to value it.

Eddie Absolutely.

Brian Never tell nowadays. Might be worth a fortune. Well, it is to *me* at the moment.

Eddie guides Brian to the Staff Rooms door

Eddie Let me know what you think as soon as you can, there's a good chap.

Brian backs out through the Staff Rooms door. It isn't easy, with the painting. He exits

Eddie closes the window

Joan Why did he have to go into the garden?

Eddie Didn't I say? I'm so sorry. (*He guides her towards the Treatment Rooms*) He's valueing the painting for me . . .

Joan *Why in the garden?*

Eddie Because of the light. Yes—the light. So much better at this time of year, don't you agree?

He ushers her into the Treatment Rooms

Joan Where are you taking me?

Eddie For some sun.

Joan In *here*?

Eddie Lamp—sun lamp—wonderful for the skin.

Joan Oh well—I suppose that while I'm here, I might as well . . .

Joan and Eddie exit.
  Minnie enters from the Staff Rooms with the dummy

Minnie opens the cupboard door. She puts the dummy into the cupboard and takes out Joan's suitcase, thinking it to be her own. As she does, she tips the pile of Brian's clothing on to the floor, but does not notice it. She opens the suitcase and reacts, surprised. She reaches in to pull out a woman's undergarment, She stares at it, uncomprehending

Mrs Court-Bending enters heartily through the main doors

Mrs Court-Bending Back again! (*She guffaws and rubs her hands*)

Minnie is still staring at the garment in her hands

I've just been in the woods for a tramp.

Minnie Did you get one?

Mrs Court-Bending Across to the jolly old Millington's place. They've got some old toys for the kiddies. Let's have 'em, I said. All in a good cause. (*Seeing the suitcase*) I see you've got it all ready for me then.

Minnie It was in the cupboard—Mr Edward must have put it there.

Mrs Court-Bending That's the spirit. Anything else?

Minnie goes to the bundle of Brian's clothing

Minnie There's only this.

Mrs Court-Bending Every little helps. (*She takes the clothing and puts it in the suitcase. She closes the lid*) Got to dash—committee meeting at six. I'll bring the case back—any other old rubbish gratefully received. All in a good cause. Cheer-oh. (*She clumps out with the suitcase, but turns at the doors*) You know—you've made someone—somewhere— jolly happy.

Mrs Court-Bending exits through the main doors

Minnie stands for a moment, her mind ticking over very slowly. Suddenly she hears voices from the garden

Joan (*off*) Where are you going *now*?

Eddie enters

Eddie I thought I heard Brian.

Eddie guiltily pulls Joan's dress from behind his back, then sees Minnie. Minnie dashes about, dusting, taking up the phones, opening the window

What are you *doing*?

Minnie Distributing myself, sir.

Eddie Well *don't*.

Minnie starts to exit sadly

Minnie!

Minnie Sir?

Eddie Get rid of this. (*He gives her Joan's dress*)

Minnie But the lady from Oxford's just been, sir.
Eddie Well—eat it yourself.

Eddie exits to the Treatment Rooms. Minnie stares at the dress, then exits by the main doors

Nancy (*off*) Brian—where are you going?

Brian enters from the Staff Rooms, still clutching the painting. He is backing upstairs when Nancy appears at the window behind him, still holding the tennis racquet

Nancy But we haven't even *started*.
Brian (*desperately*) I've got to have my plimsolls.
Nancy Can't you play barefoot—like me?
Brian I know it sounds ridiculous but I've got this thing about playing tennis without any shoes on.
Nancy You've got shoes on.
Brian Tennis shoes—plimsolls.
Nancy We'll never get started.
Brian Of course we will: you have a little stroll—I'll be with you in five minutes. (*He backs up the stairs*)

Nancy sighs and moves out of sight

Brian moves along the gallery towards Room 4

Eddie enters from the Treatment Rooms. He looks worried and goes quickly to the window. Joan enters from the Treatment Rooms, wearing a toga

Joan I'm parched. It must be that sun-lamp.

Eddie vaguely indicates the jug on the desk

Eddie There's some water on the desk.

Before he can stop her, she takes up the large glass of vodka and downs the lot

Joan That's better. (*And the spirit hits the bottom of her stomach*) It's like fire!
Eddie I'm not surprised—it's a hundred and ten per cent proof!
Joan Proof?
Eddie Prove—*im*proved—*improved*—improved *spa water*.
Joan I must say it's given me quite a pleasant glow.
Eddie Just a word of warning: if you happen to see a lighted match, don't breathe a word.
Joan Look here—Brian *must* be back by now.
Eddie Yes, he is. You just missed him.

Joan Where did he go?

Eddie Into the gymnasium. For a gym.

Joan looks at him, then exits to the Gymnasium

She never *touches* the stuff! (*He goes to the main doors*)

Brian Psst!

Eddie She *will* be. (*He looks up and sees Brian*) What *is* it?

Brian (*coming downstairs*) I can't do it—I can't do it . . .

Eddie Get a hold of yourself.

Brian *Please!*

Eddie You haven't just left her *standing* there?

Brian She's gone for a walk. I said I'd meet her. But how can I? If Joan went out there and found me—*us*—like this . . .

Eddie Joan won't be going anywhere. I've taken care of that.

Brian What have you done?

Eddie Joined the ranks of the common criminal, that's what I've done. Look I'll explain later. Go and see Nancy.

Brian I can't—don't you understand. I can't.

Eddie All right—I'll go and make some excuse to her. You go and see Joan.

Brian Thank you—thank you . . .

Eddie And hurry.

Brian I will—yes, I will. (*He is moving away when he suddenly remembers*) Where are my clothes?

Eddie What clothes?

Brian *My* clothes: I can't keep walking about like this. What if *Joan* sees me?

Eddie You're right. (*He goes to the cupboard and looks inside*) They've gone.

Brian (*eyes heavenwards*) It's a punishment—that's what it is—a punishment.

Eddie You'll have to borrow some of mine. Upstairs—in my room.

Brian But I want my *own* clothes. I *like* them.

Eddie You can have them when we *find* them. Lord knows what's happened to them. (*Ordering him*) Go and get some of mine.

Brian starts miserably upstairs again

Joan enters from the Gymnasium. The vodka is beginning to take effect on her, and throughout the following scene she pronounces her words with unusual care

Brian freezes

Joan What are you two up to?

Brian and Eddie each jerk a hand to their necks

Brian ⎫ *Here.* ⎰ *Speaking*
Eddie ⎰   ⎱ *together*

Joan (*to Brian*) I thought you were suppissed to be in the gymnausium—
   I'm sorry, I'll read that again—supposed to be in the gymernasium.
Brian I was—yes—I was.
Joan Then why *aren't* you?
Brian Because—because—*he stopped me*! (*He points accusingly at Eddie*)
   Joan (*to Eddie*) Why?
Eddie Why?
Brian Yes—why?

*Eddie looks around hopelessly. Then he realizes that he is standing by the
desk. He takes up the telephone*

Eddie Because someone wanted him on the telephone. (*To Brian*) Didn't
   they?
Brian Yes.
Joan Who?
Eddie Yes—who?
Brian Who?
Eddie }
Joan } Yes—*who*? { *Speaking*
            { *together*
Brian It was—a business call. Yes—business.
Joan What sort of business?
Brian It was—Angus. Yes—Angus McSmith! (*Triumphantly*) There's a
   panic on. They can't do without me. They need me back in London!
Eddie They can't.
Brian They can and they do!
Eddie But a move like that could be fatal. For *all* of us.
Brian They *need* me. And—sick as I am—(*he coughs*)—I must go.
Joan And *I'll* go with you.
Brian Off we go then . . . (*He moves towards the main doors*)
Joan Aren't you forgetting something?
Brian What's that?
Joan Shouldn't you put your clothes on?

*Brian looks down at the painting. Then, with full dignity, and keeping
the painting facing the audience, he crosses the stage, does a little jig to
keep the painting in the right place as he mounts the stairs, another jig
at the top, along the gallery, and a final twist of the painting lets him into
Room 4. He closes the door.*
   *Maxie enters from Room 2. He is done up like a circus strongman,
leopard-skin leotards, baggy tights, waxed moustache, an armband with
sergeant's stripes*

Maxie (*as he comes downstairs*) You and you! Fall in for acrobatics!
Eddie (*in an aside*) Not now, Maxie.
Maxie What am I supposed to *do* then?
Eddie Just—hang about—and take your cue from me.
Maxie (*puzzled*) Gymnasium—I could have sworn he said gymnasium

Maxie exits to the Gymnasium

Eddie Incredibly enthusiastic, my staff. (*He glances furtively from the window*)

Joan Then why hasn't one of them brought my shootcase up?

Eddie What shootcase? (*He pours her a vodka*)

Joan takes the glass and drinks

Joan I arrived with a shootcase and I intend to leave with a shootcase.

Eddie Are you quite sure you brought it?

Joan Absolutely. (*She points*) I left it by the desk.

Eddie I don't . . . (*He suddenly remembers*) Oh—that was *your* suitcase?

Joan What was?

Eddie The one I—I'm bringing up to your room.

He tops up her glass. She drinks

Joan You're not *up* to anything, are you?

Eddie (*totally innocent*) Up to anything? What *could* I be up to?

Joan I don't know. But whatever it is—*shop* it? And not only that—*shop* it. (*She goes upstairs, closing the window. Outside her room, she gives a little burp, puts a hand to her mouth and giggles*) Manners.

Joan exits to Room 1

Eddie goes to the window and looks out for Nancy. He turns, leaving the window open

Brian enters, still naked and with the picture

Nancy (*off*) Brian! Brian!

Nancy appears at the window

Where is he?

Brian freezes at the top of the stairs. Eddie turns and moves quickly back to the window

Eddie Isn't he in the garden?

Nancy No, he isn't. I'm fed up. I'm coming in. (*She turns*)

Eddie No! That is—the door's stuck. You know what it's like—these old houses.

Nancy Well, how am I supposed to get in?

Eddie The carpenter's on his way. As soon as he's fixed it, I'll give you a shout.

Nancy (*firmly*) I don't want a shout—I want to come in.

Eddie Yes, of course you do. Tell you what—why don't you go round the back?

Nancy moves out of sight

Eddie turns and sees Brian quivering on the stairs

Don't just stand there—she's coming in!

Brian exits quickly into Room 4. Nancy's head appears round the Staff Rooms door

Nancy Is he here?
Eddie Just gone.
Nancy Just *gone*?
Eddie (*looking at his watch*) Four o'clock. Time flies. No, he isn't.
Nancy Good.

Nancy pushes open the door. Eddie waits for the worst. But is surprised to see that Nancy is wearing one of the towelling togas

(*Referring to the toga*) Please don't tell Brian about this—I got so cold waiting for him out there.
Eddie (*relieved*) He'd understand—I'm sure he would.
Nancy Oh, you don't know him—he's such a fanatic about these things.
Eddie Oh, he *is*—he *is* . . .

The Treatment Rooms door burst open and Maxie enters, dressed as a master carpenter—flat cap, walrus moustache, sack of tools

Eddie and Nancy can only stand and watch

Maxie Where's this 'ere door then? Ah—there it is.

Maxie moves to the main doors, tosses down his tools and whips out a rule

(*Measuring the door*) Lovely bit of timber, this is. Came off an old ship, you know. They don't make doors like this any more. Fashioned with loving care by a master craftsman. (*He takes up a wooden mallet and takes several hefty swipes at the door. Then he delicately takes the handle between finger and thumb and opens the door a little. He pushes it shut*) A gem. A little gem. (*He turns to them*) You won't have no more trouble with that, guvnor.
Eddie Thank you—Walter. (*He pushes Maxie back towards the Treatment Rooms*)
Maxie That's me, miss—Walter Stain—Master Carpenter for all occasions . . .
Eddie (*in an aside*) Calm yourself—take a pill . . .

Eddie gets Maxie into the Treatment Rooms

Nancy goes to the window and closes it

Nancy Not very warm in here, is it?

Eddie It's the heating. I'm having it fixed.

Nancy Will it be long?

Eddie A trice. There's a whole army of engineers working on it.

> *The main doors burst open and Minnie enters carrying a huge spanner. She curtsies, then crosses to thump one of the radiators with the spanner, then moves back to the door, curtsies again, and exits to the Gym*

Nancy I suppose that was the Brigadier?

> *The Treatment Rooms door opens and Maxie enters—dressed as an army officer*

Maxie Somebody call?

Eddie Oh God! I mean—ah! Brigadier Knutsford-Browne.

Maxie (*to Nancy*) Royal Army Catering Corps.

Eddie *Catering* Corps?

Maxie Central Eating.

Eddie (*between clenched teeth*) *Heating*.

Maxie Quite so, old chap. Heaving Advisor to the Royal Army Catering Corps. God! It's hell in there!

> *Maxie exits to the Treatment Rooms*

Eddie (*to Nancy*) You see? Everything's under control. Why don't you pop into the sauna? That'll warm you up.

Nancy I think I will.

> *Nancy exits to the Treatment Rooms.*
> *Brian enters from Room 4, naked, with the picture, and looks over the balcony*

Brian (*coming downstairs*) Where is she?

Eddie (*pointing to the Treatment Rooms*) In there. Where are your clothes?

Brian I haven't *got* any clothes.

Eddie Well, put mine on—in my room—you're supposed to be in London.

Brian London? Oh, yes—so I am. (*He breaks down at his hopeless plight*) I can't go on—I can't go on . . .

Joan (*off*) Where is my husband?

> *At the sound of Joan's voice, Eddie bundles Brian into the Staff Rooms. Joan enters, coming downstairs. Her drunkenness has increased*

Joan Where'sh my husband?

Eddie Looking for *you*.

Joan Looking for *me*?

Eddie Didn't he find you?

Joan No. Where'sh he gone?

Eddie (*pointing*) To the Treatment Rooms. For a treat.

Joan exits to the Treatment Rooms

Joan (*as she goes, giggling*) To the Treatment Roomsh—for a treat . . .

Brian enters from the Staff Rooms. He is wearing a cap and overall identical to Minnie's. He comes on backwards, watched by the astonished Eddie. When they are face to face, Brian curtsies.
Joan enters from the Treatment Rooms

Brian, turns his back on her and "does a Minnie", curtsies, dusts, etc.

Joan Where is he?
Eddie Who?
Joan Brian.
Eddie Brian? Which Brian?
Joan Are you praying games?
Eddie Praying games? What a good idea. You go into the garden and I won't come and find you.
Joan (*wagging her finger*) Are you shaying he's in the garden?
Eddie I am—yes—I am . . .
Joan I shuppose he's gone for a *guard*?

Joan giggles and exits to the Staff Rooms

Eddie (*to Brian*) Get those things off!

Brian exits to the Gymnasium

Brian, bewildered, goes to mount the stairs

Minnie enters from the Treatment Rooms, minus her spectacles

Minnie Oh, sir—oh, sir—I've lost my spectacles, sir

Brian and Minnie come face to face. They go into a double-Minnie routine —polishing a mirror between them, etc.

Brian makes an exit through the upstairs alcove

Minnie stands, trying to work things out. She opens the window and waves air over herself

Eddie enters from the Gymnasium

Eddie I thought I told you to get those clothes off!

At the sound of his voice, Minnie smiles coyly and starts to unbutton her overall

Minnie I *was* saving myself for my pirate, sir . . . but anything you say . . .
Eddie (*realizing and stopping her*) No, no, Minnie—my mistake.

Minnie stops, disappointed

Minnie I think I've been over-distributing myself, sir. I don't know
whether I'm coming or going. I'm sure I just went—but I can't have—
because I'm just going . . . (*She moves to the Treatment Rooms door*) I've
lost my spectacles, sir.
Eddie They can't be far. Go and look for them.
Minnie Yes, sir.

> *Still confused, Minnie exits to the Treatment Rooms.*
> *Joan enters from the Staff Rooms*

Joan He's not in the garden.
Eddie He's gone to London.
Joan Well, of all the—juss a minute—his car's still there.
Eddie He took the train. Yes. The train. That's why he had to dash off.
To catch the train.
Joan What's wrong with the car?
Eddie I don't know. That is—*no-one* knows. We've had the A.A., the
R.A.C., they can't understand it. It's a complete mystery.

> *Maxie enters from the Treatment Rooms—dressed as a railway official
> with lamp, whistle and flag. He gives a short blast on the whistle*

Eddie puts a despairing hand to his face

Maxie Which one of you two gentlemen is Mrs Manchip?
Joan I'm Mrs Manchip.
Maxie I have a message from your late husband.

Eddie		
	Late?	Speaking
Joan		together

Maxie Late for the train, that is. Luckily we was delayed. The message
reads: See You Soon: Your Loving Husband, Mr Manchip.
Eddie It's very good of you to come . . . (*He pushes Maxie towards the
Treatment Rooms door*)
Maxie Not at all, sir. As I say, there's a slight delay due to cattle on the
line. However, we're doing our best. (*He blows his whistle*)

> *Eddie helps Maxie through the door*

Joan stares after him

Eddie Incredibly obliging, these locals.
Joan I think I'll have a little lay-doon on my bread. (*She goes shakily upstairs, closing the window en route*)

Brian exits quickly to Room 4

Joan Edward—where is my sitcuss?

Eddie Your sitcuss?

Joan I'm so sorry—I seem to be having trouble with my vowels. (*With great care*) My sit—cuss.

Eddie Oh, yes—of course. Your suitcase. Just coming.

Joan And my dresh.

Eddie What dress?

Joan I left it downstairs. Have someone bring it up.

Eddie And I'll get you some blankets.

Joan exits to Room 1. After a moment, Brian comes warily out of the upstairs alcove. He wears Eddie's suit, which is much too big for him

Eddie motions for him to come down quickly. But Brian comes down the stairs in a state of nervous exhaustion

Brian Look at me? What am I supposed to be doing?

Eddie You're supposed to be in London.

Brian looks around gratefully

Brian Dear old London. (*Suddenly animated*) How can I be in London? I'm playing tennis. I *hate* tennis. (*He grabs Eddie*) I'm ill—don't you understand—*ill*.

The Treatment Rooms door bursts open and Maxie enters—dressed as a cowboy. He is making bad passes with a lassoo

Maxie Where's this here hornery cow?

Brian (*jerking his head around*) What cow—what cow?

Maxie (*in his normal voice*) The cow that's holding up the train.

Brian What train?

Eddie The train *you're* on.

Brian Am I on a train? I *like* trains . . .

Maxie (*as a cowboy again*) Remember back in fifty-four—President's train comin' through and a herd of buffalo chewin' up the track. Jake, they said—Jake . . .

Brian (*astonished*) Who *is* he?

Eddie Maxie? He's here to help clean up the mess you've made.

Brian *I've* made?

Eddie Don't boast about it.

Maxie (*gulping pills*) How'm I doing?

Eddie Words fail me.

Brian (*suddenly annoyed*) I refuse to take part in this any longer. (*He moves to the stairs*)

Eddie Where are you going?

Brian To see my wife. I shall explain the whole affair to her. She'll understand. We shall then kiss and make up . . .

Eddie (*derisive*) Kiss and make up . . . (*Realizing*) Makeup! That's it! (*He moves to the cupboard and takes out the wheelchair*)

Brian (*looking around, bewildered*) What is?
Eddie You don't have to go to *London*—you don't have to go *anywhere*.

He pushes Brian down into the chair

    Maxie's a make-up expert—he can turn you into an old man.
Brian I *am* an old man.
Eddie No-one will recognize you—it's perfect—do your stuff, Maxie . . .
(*He pushes the chair across to Maxie*)
Brian trying to protest) Edward, I would like to consider this matter more fully . . .
Eddie Certainly. I'll go and get the two ladies. We can *all* consider it.

Brian raises an admonishing finger, but instead turns to look up at Maxie

Brian (*meekly*) I see myself as Schweitzer rather than Churchill, don't you?

Maxie wheels Brian out through the Staff Rooms door

Eddie rubs hands together, pleased with himself

    Joan enters from Room 1

Joan (*over the balcony, woozily*) I want to telephone London.
Eddie Certainly. What number? (*He moves to take up the telephone*)
Joan *My* number.
Eddie But you're *here*.
Joan So I am. Why am I phoning myself? Oh, yes—I want to speak to Brian.
Eddie Of course. (*He dials, but slaps the receiver down*) You can't. That is, he won't be there yet.
Joan Well, keep trying until he *is*. And bring me up a glash of that imsparred proof-water.

    Joan exits to Room 1. Mr Butcher enters through main doors

Eddie turns, sees him, and nearly jumps out of his skin

Eddie I *wish* you wouldn't do that, Mr Butcher.
Mr Butcher Do what, Eddie boy?
Eddie Come in.
Mr Butcher Very witty, Eddie boy—very very witty. As a matter of fact, I've just been on the blower to the guvnor telling him how witty you was —he was particularly amused by your little joke about not being able to raise the ready. Oh, we *did* have a good laugh.

Mr Butcher "laughs". Eddie nervously joins in

    Yus. You've endeared yourself to him. Tell my friend Eddie the Elf I don't *want* this house, he said.

Eddie Did he really? How very reasonable.

Mr Butcher Yus. Tell him I'll settle for the straight twenty thousand, he said. That must be a weight off your mind, Eddie boy.

Eddie Enormous.

Mr Butcher Just make sure it don't end up round your feet.

Eddie "laughs" nervously

That's what I like, Eddie, a man who laughs in the face of death. So don't keep me hanging about, Eddie—I'm missing the Galloping Gourmet. Got quite a nice technique with the cleaver, that boy . . .

The main doors open and a uniformed Police Sergeant enters

Mr Butcher is clearly perturbed and examines a poster studiously

Sergeant Hello, hello, hello. What's all this, then? Hanging about when danger lurks not fifty yards away? Stand still—and be prepared to answer a few pertinent and, though I says it myself, frighteningly incisive questions.

Eddie Officer. How nice to see you—how very, very, *very* nice to see you.

Sergeant (*referring to Mr Butcher*) Who's this, then?

Eddie This? Oh, this is Mr Butcher—from the card school—*old* school— the headmaster of my old school. Just popped in to say hello.

Mr Butcher Yus. (*He clears his throat*) 'Ullo, Eddie.

Eddie 'Ullo, Headmaster.

Mr Butcher Yus. Well—can't 'ang abaht—gotta get back to the old school like.

Sergeant Eton?

Mr Butcher I'll have a bite on the way. (*He moves to the door*) I'll be in touch. And don't forget your donation towards clearing out the school gravel pit, there's a good boy.

Mr Butcher exits

Eddie sighs with relief

Eddie God bless you, officer. What can I do for you?

Sergeant We have received a complaint from the Chief Constable's wife —Mrs Court-Bending. You probably know the lady in another capacity —that of a most prominent welfare worker.

Eddie Do I?

Sergeant She was here only today, as a matter of fact. Collecting discarded garments for the starving masses in the City of Oxford.

Eddie (*remembering*) Oh—yes—of course—charming lady.

Sergeant As she was leaving these premises and perambulating in a somewhat south-westerly direction, she happened to perceive what she has subsequently described as a naked female form of infinite proportion leaping about in your shrubbery . . .

Eddie (*worried*) Nancy . . .

Sergeant I beg your pardon?

Eddie Granted. She must have been seeing things . . .

Sergeant Exactly what Mrs Court-Bending thought herself. However, any doubts were instantly dispelled when the apparition turned a double somersault and disappeared into the foliage with a cry of: (*He refers to his notebook*) "Get your clothes off and live." (*He shuts the notebook*) This as you know, sir, is an outrage against public decency and nine hundred and thirty-four officers of the law have given up their leave to hunt down the brazen hussy. I take it you know nothing of this affair, sir?

Eddie No—no—nothing at all. (*He backs protectively towards the Treatment Rooms door, spreading his arms against it to stop anyone coming through*)

Sergeant I don't have to remind you, sir, that the arm of the law is long and relentless and, as a matter of fact—(*he touches his nose delicately as a reminder*)—it's getting rather thirsty.

Eddie My dear fellow. Why don't you pop through into the kitchen and have yourself a nice pot of tea. (*He winks*) Or something a little stronger. (*He indicates the Staff door*)

Sergeant Thank you, sir. I don't mind if I do. (*He takes off his helmet and moves towards the Staff Rooms door*) Thirsty work this relentless hunting.

The Staff Rooms door opens and Maxie—in white coat and stethescope— pushes in Brian in the wheelchair. Brian is made up like an old man. The wig is covered in flour. He is huddled under blankets. A huge ear trumpet rests on his lap

Maxie (*in a heavy "German" accent*) Ve are shust goink for our valk in zer garten. Auf wiener-schnitzel.

Sergeant Take my advice and be very careful who you bump into. (*He takes up the ear trumpet and bellows into Brian's ear*) Not that it'll do *you* much good, eh?

The Sergeant laughs merrily, then collects his dignity, replaces the trumpet and marches, policeman-wise, through the Staff Rooms door

Brian (*rubbing his aching ear*) What's he talking about?

Eddie (*furtively*) I don't know.

Brian What's he doing here?

Eddie He—er—just popped in for a cup of tea.

Maxie (*indicating Brian*) What d'you think of him?

Eddie Marvellous, Maxie. His own sister wouldn't recognize him.

Brian I haven't got a sister.

Eddie Then we're that much safer.

Maxie Who's he remind you of?

Eddie No idea.

Maxie It's my Uncle Fred, in'it?

Brian suddenly leaps to his feet, sending up a shower of white dust

Brian I don't *care* about your Uncle Fred. I'm on the nerve of a vergous breakdown and what do you do? (*He bangs his wigged head, sending up a cloud of flour*) Sprinkle me with flour. All it needs to do now is *rain* and you'll have a Yorkshire pudding on your hands. Three hours ago I was a happily married man with a flourishing business. *Now* look at me. A potential Yorkshire pudding on the verge of a nervous breakdown. I can't stand it—don't you understand? I can't stand it, I tell you . . . (*He stands up and repeats "I can't stand it, I tell you . . ." while at the same time angrily stamping his foot*)

Nancy enters from the Treatment Rooms, unseen by Brian

Immediately, Eddie takes up the chant with Brian and turns it into la-la-ing "The Mexican Hat Dance". He grabs Nancy and whirls her round to the tune. Maxie gets the idea and whirls Brian round—all of them now dancing to the tune. They finish with a posed "Olé!". Then Brian slumps back into the wheelchair and takes up his ear-trumpet

Nancy (*to Eddie*) That *was* fun.
Eddie Wasn't it?
Nancy (*seeing Brian*) Oh, hello. (*To Eddie*) Another guest?
Eddie Just arrived. He's incommunicado. (*Shouting at Brian*) Aren't you, Colonel?
Brian (*protesting*) No, I'm not!
Eddie (*pointedly*) Only *his* wife is just like *your* husband. If she ever finds out he comes to a place like this . . .

Brian takes the point and gropes shakily for his ear trumpet

Brian Eh? Eh? What's that? Eh?
Nancy He *is* a nudist?
Eddie Oh, *yes*.
Nancy It doesn't seem to have done him much good.
Eddie It worked all right for the first ninety-five years—(*shouting*)—didn't it, Colonel?
Nancy (*to Eddie*) Where's Brian?
Eddie He's—er—he's gone for a swim.
Nancy What a lovely idea—I think I'll join him.

Nancy moves to the main doors and exits

Eddie She can't go out *there*.
Brian Why not?
Eddie They've given up their leave . . . nine hundred and thirty-four of 'em.
Brian Nine hundred and thirty-four *what*?

Suddenly Nancy's toga comes fluttering through the door and wraps around Eddie's head. He tries to disentangle himself

Joan enters from Room 1

Joan What about my call to London?

Brian cowers behind the blankets

Eddie I was just doing it. (*He dashes to the desk and dials a number. He listens a moment, then slams the phone down*) No answer.

Joan He mush be there by now—unlesh he's up to his tricksh again—let me try. (*She comes shakily downstairs*)

Eddie No, no, I'll do it—no point in wearing out your fingers when you should be resting—(*he dials feverishly*)—oh, Brian, it's me . . . (*Pointedly*) Joan wants to make sure you've arrived. You'd better speak to her.

Brian is horrified. As Joan moves past him he gesticulates furiously at Eddie who ignores him. Eddie holds out the phone towards Joan. As she reaches for it he switches it to his other arm and holds it at arm's length so that she has to move to the other side of the desk to take hold of it. As soon as she takes hold of the phone Eddie dashes across to the wall phone beside the Staff Rooms door. He takes it off the hook and hands it to Brian indicating that he can speak to Joan through it

Joan (*into the receiver*) Hello? Hello?

Brian realizes and speaks into the receiver

Brian Hello?

Joan You sound very near, dear.

Brian shoots out his arm so that he is holding the phone as far away as possible

Brian Do I really, dearie?

Joan Very near indeedy, sweedy.

Brian It must be——

Eddie squeezes Brian's nose to produce a nasal tone

   —an exceptionally good line

Joan It was. It isn't *now*.

Brian holds his own nose

Brian How nice of you to phone.

Joan Yes. I wanted you to do something for me.

Brian Anything—anything . . .

Joan When you come back, I want you to bring some closhe for me.

Brian Closhe?

Joan Some of my warm closhe. I didn't bring any with me and I'm boozing. I mean froozing.

Eddie She means freezing.

Brian But I can't!

Joan Why not?

Brian Because—because—how do I know what you want?

Joan Jush look in my wardrobe and fesh the warmesh thingsh you can find. Good-bri, Byan. (*She puts down the receiver*)

Brian But I'm ill—don't you understand—*ill*.

Joan Yesh, darling—and your little Joany-woany is going to . . . (*Suddenly it strikes her. She looks down at the telephone. Then up again*)

Eddie claps a hand over Brian's mouth. Joan turns—Eddie whips his hand away

He'sh here.

Eddie Who?

Joan Bry Mian.

Eddie Bry Mian?

Joan I *heard* him.

Eddie Not Bry *Mian*.

Joan *Who* then?

Eddie Who? (*He points at Maxie*) Him.

Joan (*to Maxie*) Who are you?

Maxie Who am I?

Eddie } Yes—who *are* you? { *Speaking*
Joan }   { *together*

Maxie is bewildered

Maxie (*in a "German" accent*) Allow me to introduce mein selbst. (*He clicks his heels*) Ludwig Kernock—female impersonator extra-ordinary. (*He clears his throat*) Ze cuckoo. (*He puts his hands to his mouth and does a bad bird impersonation*) Ach—listen—here kommt faissful Rover who ist ze sheep gebringen. (*He clears his throat and does a bad dog and sheep impersonation*) Voof, voof—ba—ba—gut dog Rover. (*He pats a non-existent dog*)

Joan turns to the cowering Brian

Joan And who's *thish*?

Eddie Thish? Thish is his dummy.

Maxie Ja—mein dummy. *Dummy?*

Eddie For your ventriloquist act.

Maxie (*catching on*) Ach—ja—for mein ventriloquist act. (*Indicating Brian*) Ziss ist der Archduke Andrews.

Joan (*suspiciously*) If you're a bentbigamist—let me see you go bent. (*She looks at Eddie*)

Eddie *Yes*.

Maxie Mit pleasure. (*He moves grandly across to take up a chair and set it alongside the wheelchair*) I just bent to get the chair.

Maxie takes Brian by the collar and "lifts" him out of the wheelchair so that Maxie sits on the chair with Brian on his lap.

Brian—in desperate fear of his wife—goes along with the act—limbs hanging limply from his over-large suit—his face assuming a puppet-like insane grin

Vy—hello—mein little vooden-headed friend. Vot have you been doink today?

Brian is paralyzed with fear, having no idea what a ventriloquist dummy would say or do

Brian Help!

Maxie seizes his neck and screws his head round so that they are face to face

Maxie I said . . .

Brian nods feverishly. He puts on a fixed smile and his eyes jerk wildly from side to side

Brian (*as the dummy*) I heard what you said.
Maxie Then answer—dumpkopf!
Brian You're working well tonight.
Maxie If you don't answer . . .
Brian A gockle of geer—a gockle of geer . . .
Maxie Ve have vays of making you talk . . .
Brian Look at me when you're talking—look at me . . .
Maxie Take zat stupid grin off your face . . .
Brian I can see your lips moving . . .
Joan Oh thish is ridilicous! You're drunk—thas what you are—drunk!

Joan staggers upstairs and into her room

Maxie has become lost in "characterization". He grabs Brian by the throat and starts to throttle him. Eddie tries to pull him off

Maxie Ze fuhrer vill hear of your insolence! Vere ver you on ze night of ze sixteenth? Who is your contact? Vere ist der radio equipment . . . ?

Eddie gets Brian free. Brian leaps to his feet. Maxie staggers round in a trance

Brian Finished! No more! I've suffered enough of you, understand! (*He begins ripping off the clothes, hurling them and the wig away*)
Maxie Who am I? Where am I? What am I *doing*?
Brian From now on—the truth! I am a fully certified chartered accountant and I will endure no more. Finished! (*By now he is stripped down to underpants and vest. He hurls the last item of Eddie's clothing to the floor*)
Nancy (*off*) Brian!
Brian (*instantly*) Coming! (*He prances across to the window like a young nymph, and dives head first through it*)

Maxie and Eddie stand stock-still, as—

the CURTAIN *falls*

ACT II

A few minutes later

When the CURTAIN *rises, Eddie is discovered pacing back and forth. Brian, still in his "old man" guise, "paces" back and forth in the wheelchair. From outside is heard a chorus of police whistles*

Brian Come on then—astound me—let's have another of your *brilliant* ideas.

Eddie How do you feel about a suicide pact?

Brian Oh—very *good*—how would you suggest we go about it?

Eddie Well—*you* could bore yourself to death and *I* could jump out of a window.

Brian *You*—you haven't got the *courage*.

Eddie How dare you? What about when I was in the Upper Sixth and Prudence Blenkinsop refused to marry me? How many hours was I on that window ledge before the police dragged me in?

Brian It was a bungalow.

Eddie The thought was there.

Brian And you weren't *standing* on that window-sill, you were *sitting* on it, facing inwards, chewing an apple and watching television.

Eddie Well—the Lone Ranger was on.

Brian Enough of this, Edward! Now you listen to *me*—Joan thinks I'm ill—not only that, she thinks I'm in London—not only that, she wants me to fetch some of her clothes back. But this, my dear brother, is proving a little difficult because I'm a hundred and three years old and in a wheelchair. Sort *that* out.

Eddie The answer seems fairly obvious.

Brian Well?

Eddie You're in a terrible mess.

Brian Then you might also care to run your mind over the woman out there hunting down a naked policeman—I mean naked ventriloquist— I mean I'm going mad. (*He buries his head in his hands*)

Eddie Of course there's an *alternative*.

Brian Well?

Eddie We could do what every other full-blooded member of our family has done when his back's against the wall.

Brian What's that?

Eddie Emigrate.

Nancy appears at the open window

Nancy (*calling*) Hello?

The two men react. Brian cringes under the blanket: Eddie moves to the window

Eddie (*brightly*) Ah—there you are.

Nancy Is there a football ground near here?

Eddie Not that I know of—why?

Nancy I keep hearing men shouting and blowing whistles.

Eddie (*worried*) The police.

Nancy Police?

Eddie Police Training School. Where they train policemen. To—shout. And blow whistles.

Nancy How fascinating.

Eddie Isn't it? Don't you think it would be a good idea to come in?

Nancy Why?

Eddie All that noise.

Nancy I don't mind. (*She makes to move away, then turns*) I thought you said Brian was having a swim.

Eddie Yes.

Nancy He's not in the pool—I've looked.

Eddie Ah. Did you look *under* the water?

Nancy *Under* it?

Eddie Incredible underwater swimmer, Brian. Stays down for *hours*.

Nancy I didn't think of that.

Eddie I'm glad *I* did.

Nancy I'll have a look.

Eddie Good idea.

Nancy exits

Brian How can I go swimming! I'm up to my neck in it as it *is* . . .

Eddie I've had an idea.

Brian Whatever it is—*no*.

Eddie We'll borrow *her* clothes.

Brian Who, *her*?

Eddie Nancy. She doesn't need them—Joan *does*. Simple.

Brian Simple he says. (*He buries his face in his hands*)

Eddie Room Number Three—quick—before Joan comes out. Which reminds me—I said I'd get her some extra blankets.

Brian sighs and stands up. He pulls off the wig and blankets and tosses them into the wheelchair

Brian (*going upstairs*) It would have been easier to rob a bank—that's what I should have done—robbed a bank . . .

Brian exits to Room 3

Eddie wheels the chair into the cupboard. He closes the door and goes to get himself a drink

Mr Butcher enters, worried, through the main doors

Mr Butcher Come 'ere, you—what's your game? The place is swarming with coppers.

Eddie Ah—Mr Butcher. Run out of trees?

Mr Butcher reaches out a huge hand and slaps it on top of Eddie's head. His grip tightens; Eddie's knees sag

Mr Butcher Have you grassed?

Eddie Not me: it must be the dog.

Mr Butcher I ought to crack your skull.

Joan enters from Room 1 and moves to the balcony, holding a damp towel to her head

Joan Edward . . . (*She winces at the sound of her voice*)

Mr Butcher releases his grip on Eddie

Mr Butcher I've got to keep out of sight.

Eddie Go into . . . (*His voice has gone. He starts again*) Go into the sauna bath.

Mr Butcher They might follow me in there.

Eddie No—their buttons would go rusty.

Mr Butcher Not a word, you understand—not a word.

Mr Butcher exits quickly to the Treatment Rooms

Eddie touches his poor head

Joan (*coming part of the way downstairs*) Who was that?

Eddie That? Oh—that was Mr Butcher.

Joan Why was he touching your head?

Eddie That's his job, you see: he puts the finger on people.

Joan You mean he's a faith healer?

Eddie A fai . . . That's it—yes. Mr Healer The Faith Butcher—I mean, Mr Butcher The Faith Healer. You're quite right, yes. Yes. Absolutely. What can I do for you?

Joan Those blankets.

Eddie On their way.

Joan moves towards her room

Joan My God, Edward, that spa water was strong.

Eddie Puts hair on your chest.

Joan What?

Eddie I'd wear a thick vest.

Joan I *never* wear a vest.

Eddie Of course you do: what about when Brian bought you that black négligée?

Joan What about it?

Eddie Well, I remember how excited he was when he could see your vest through it.

Joan Did he tell you *that*?

Eddie Not really—it's just that he's in enough trouble and I can't see that a little more will make any difference.

Joan (*angrily*) Oh . . .

Joan goes up to Room 1 and exits, slamming the door. Minnie enters from the Staff Rooms with a pile of blankets

Eddie Who are those for?

Minnie The lady in Room One, sir.

Eddie I'll take them.

Minnie Yes, sir.

Minnie gives him the blankets and exits to the Treatment Rooms

Eddie moves to the stairs

Brian comes out of Room 3 carrying a pile of Nancy's clothing

Brian and Eddie go to the stairs together

Sergeant (*off; loudly*) Keep moving, lads—and keep your eyes open! Remember—she's starkers!

Nancy (*off*) Brian? Brian?

Brian scuttles into Room 4

Eddie jerks his head from the window to the main doors, aware of the danger. He dashes to the window

Nancy appears at the window and Brian puts a hat from the hatstand on her head

Eddie Put this on—mustn't catch a cold in the head.

The Sergeant enters from the main doors, minus his helmet

Sergeant And now, sir—to continue my relentless search for this naked felon. (*Noticing Nancy*) Afternoon, miss. You haven't by any chance seen—how shall I put it—someone out there in the garden, have you?

Nancy No, I haven't, officer. I've been searching all afternoon.

Sergeant Good work, miss. Keep it up.

Nancy I'm just coming in, as a matter of fact.

Eddie No! (*But he is too late*)

Nancy moves from the window

Eddie closes the window. The Sergeant moves towards the Staff Rooms door

(*Suddenly*) Your hat!
Sergeant What's that, sir?
Eddie Your hat—you've forgotten your hat.

The Sergeant examines the top of his head

Sergeant So I have. Silly Billy me.

The Sergeant moves ponderously across and exits through the main doors

Eddie snatches up one of the blankets and hurries to the Staff Rooms door, unfolding it

Nancy enters

Eddie drapes the blanket across her, so that she is wearing it and the large hat

Eddie Don't move! (*He holds the blanket against her and admires her as though she were a model in a new gown*)

Nancy tolerates it for a moment

Nancy What are you doing?
Eddie Doing? I'm—I'm . . .

Maxie enters grandly from the Treatment Rooms—dressed as a French couturier

Maxie (*in a "French" accent*) M'sieur Eddie is assisting moi—Henri le Bra. (*He bows*)
Eddie ("*whispering*" *to Nancy*) The famous French couturier.
Nancy (*flattered*) Oh . . .

Maxie moves across and, with Eddie's help, guides Nancy to the middle of the room

Maxie It is—how you say—magnifique. However—a little 'ere—a little there . . . (*He makes couturier passes at the blanket and produces a large safety pin to fasten the blanket across Nancy's shoulders*)

The Sergeant enters—now wearing his helmet—from the main doors

Eddie (*indicating Nancy*) What do you think, officer?
Sergeant Very nice if I may so, sir—very nice indeed. Mind you, you've got to have the body to wear that sort of thing, I always say. Put it on my old woman and it would look like a blanket. A horse blanket to boot. Which I would very much like to do. (*He bends his knees, police-man-wise*) I shall be back, sir, with, I hope, a satisfactory conclusion to this affair. Afternoon, all.

Telephone.

The Sergeant exits through the main doors

Nancy considers for a moment

Nancy What was a policeman doing here?
Eddie What an intelligent question. Tell her, M'sieur Henri.
Maxie Me? I mean—moi! Certainment. 'E was, how you say—guarding my collection.
Eddie Of course he was—guarding my collection. *His* collection.
Nancy I see. (*A thought*) But what were you doing in the gym?
Maxie Gym and I—are just good friends.

Maxie blows a precious kiss and exits to the Gymnasium

Eddie, behind Nancy's back, mops his brow

Nancy I don't understand it.
Eddie Don't try—please—don't try.
Nancy I mean—where Brian is. (*She opens the window and looks out*)
Eddie He's probably hiding—he can be very playful.
Nancy This may sound silly—but he isn't avoiding me, is he?
Eddie Avoiding you? Ridiculous.

Nancy sighs and—before Eddie can stop her—exits through the Staff Rooms door.
Mr Butcher enters from the Treatment Rooms. He is naked apart from a towel round his waist, a shoulder holster, and his hat. (Mr Butcher never removes his hat.) He is sweating profusely from the sauna bath

Mr Butcher Is the coast clear?
Eddie I don't know what it's like at the seaside but there's a deep depression centred over *this* area.
Mr Butcher The *law*.
Eddie Oh, *that* coast. No, it isn't. Stay in the sauna bath.

Mr Butcher puffs up his cheeks at the thought of it and exits to the Treatment Rooms

The telephone on the desk rings. Eddie answers it

(*Into the receiver*) Hello? . . . (*Puzzled*) Who is that? I can't hear you—why are you whispering?

The door to Room 4 bursts open and Brian appears, holding a telephone to his ear

Brian (*loudly*) I said—*what am I supposed to do now?*

The door to Room 1 opens and Joan comes out. Immediately, Brian exits to Room 4

Joan (*moving to the balcony*) Who are you talking to?
Eddie (*panicking*) Brian.
Joan Let me speak to him.
Eddie (*slamming down the receiver*) Too late.
Joan What did he want?
Eddie He was phoning to say he—he's on his way back.
Joan Thank God for that. I still haven't got my suitcase.
Eddie So you haven't.
Joan And where are those blankets?
Eddie Just coming.

Joan exits to Room 1

Eddie hurriedly picks up the blankets he has dropped. As he is doing so, the hat and blanket Nancy was wearing flutter through the window. Eddie hurries to the window but is too late to stop Nancy. He scoops up all the blankets and dashes upstairs to Room 1. He knocks on the door. Joan answers it. He thrusts the blankets into her arms and the hat on her head

There.
Joan I don't need a *hat*.
Eddie Of course you do. Keep your head warm.

Eddie ushers her into the room and closes the door. He takes a deep breath, then hurries downstairs to take up the telephone and dial a single number

(*Into the receiver*) Brian . . . You can come back from London now— with those clothes. (*He quickly replaces the receiver, then goes to look anxiously out of the window and closes it*)

Brian enters from Room 4, wearing Eddie's suit and carrying the bundle of Nancy's clothing

Eddie does not hear him

Brian Psst!

Eddie jumps

Eddie Not any more—more's the pity. (*Suddenly angry*) Don't *do* that!
Brian She's no fool, you know.
Eddie Of course she isn't. *Who*?
Brian Joan. (*Indicating the clothes*) She'll know these aren't hers.
Eddie Tell her—tell her—why do you have to be so *difficult*?

They glare at each other

Angus (*off*) Anybody about?
Eddie Who's that?

Brian (*shocked*) It's Angus!

Eddie Who's Angus?

Brian *Her* Angus—Nancy—her husband!

Eddie Oh Gawd!

Brian He's the one I'm supposed to be seeing in London!

Eddie Oh *two* Gawds.

Brian What can he *want*?

Eddie How do *I* know? He's supposed to be adjudicating porridge.

Brian He must have found out she's here—*how*?

Eddie The law of averages—*everyone's* here!

Brian What are we going to do? . . . Get rid of him!

Brian dashes upstairs and into Room 4, before Eddie can stop him.
    Angus enters through the main doors. He's very tall, wears a tam-o'-shanter and kilt. A po-faced Scot, with a briefcase

Angus Good day.

Eddie *Good day?* You must be out of your mind—that is—I mean—what can I do for you?

Angus My name's McSmith.

Eddie I know.

Angus You *knew*?

Eddie That is—I knew you were a Scotsman. As soon as I saw you getting out of that car, kilt-first, I said to myself: there's a Scotsman if ever I saw one, I said. (*He moves closer, speaking confidentially*) Tell me, old man—is anything worn under the kilt?

Angus No—everything's in perfect working condition.

Eddie Good—well—sorry you can't stay. (*He shakes Angus's hand*) I'll ring for a car . . .

Angus stands open-mouthed as Eddie takes up the receiver and immediately puts it down again

Engaged. (*He beams at Angus, then again pumps his hand*) Jolly nice meeting you. I've so enjoyed our little chat. (*All the time he guides Angus back towards the main doors*) *You* take the high road and *I'll* take the low road and, God willing, we'll never meet again . . .

Eddie bundles Angus out of the main doors, sighs, and hurries out to the Treatment Rooms.
    There is silence for a moment, then the main doors are pushed open and Angus comes back in, standing just inside

Angus (*totally perplexed*) *You* take the high road—(*he points*)—and *I'll* take the low road—(*he points to himself*)—no, *I'll* take the high road—and—what sort of place *is* this? (*He goes towards the Treatment Rooms, then suddenly stops and, with a furtive glance round, moves to the telephone and gingerly lifts the receiver. He starts to dial, whistling softly*)

Minnie enters from the Gymnasium

Immediately, Angus bangs down the receiver and starts to whistle tunelessly "You Take the High Road . . ." Minnie cocks an ear, stares around blindly, and joins in the whistling. They stand, without looking at each other, and whistle a chorus of the song

As soon as they stop, Minnie bursts into tears and dashes off into the Treatment Rooms

Angus shakes his head as though bringing himself to his senses, then, glancing round furtively again, takes up the telephone to dial. He waits, then speaks into the receiver

Angus (*in a whisper*) It's me—Angus—I've arrived. (*Looking appraisingly around*) From the look of the place, I'll be able to pick it up dirt cheap . . . No, they won't argue . . . I know from his brother that they're in dire financial straits . . . No, I won't make an offer straightaway—I'll bide my time—see what sort of man I'm dealing with . . . Are you out of your mind? I hate places like this—depraved narcissistic nonsense. I'll just have to see it through. And remember—tell no-one I'm here— word gets around I'm interested and the price goes up. Not even Nancy. As far as she's concerned, I'm still up to my neck in porridge. (*He jerks his head round as he hears Eddie calling*)

Eddie (*off*) Leave it to me, Mr Butcher—I'll find out what they're up to . . .

Angus I'll phone you later . . . (*He slaps down the receiver and crosses quickly to the window to open it and inhale deeply*)

Eddie enters from the Treatment Rooms, carrying the pile of Mr Butcher's clothing. He is in a state of fear-laden hysteria and doesn't see Angus as he throws the clothes over a chair and frantically searches through them

Eddie (*to himself*) Where's that I O U? I've got to find that I O U.

Angus clears his throat heavily. Eddie leaps away from the clothing

I was just taking your suit to the cleaners, Mr Butcher—see if they could get the bloodstains out . . . (*Realizing*) Oh—it's *you* . . . I thought you'd gone—that is—why *haven't* you *gone*?

Angus I so enjoyed my last little visit, I thought I'd pay you a return call.

Eddie But—(*he gropes for words*)—but this is a *health* farm—health. (*He puffs up his chest, doing little jiggy exercises*)

Angus Aye. (*He takes a deep breath*) Smell that air—smell that health.

Angus joins in Eddie's jigging. They carry on for a moment before Eddie stops suddenly

Eddie But you *hate* health farms!

Angus (*suspiciously*) Who said so?

Eddie *You* did—that is, you *look* like a man who hates health—that is, farms—that is—don't you?

Angus Mind you—if I thought it was one of those *camps*—you know—*nudists.*

Eddie Camp nudists—*never!*

Angus There's too much of this worshipping the human body—I don't mind telling you—people go too *far*—my own *wife* had a yen for it.

Eddie Nancy!

Angus How do you know her name?

Eddie Whose name?

Angus Nancy. You said "Nancy".

Eddie I said "fancy": fancy you having a wife called Nancy.

Angus The thought of her running around with no clothes on drives me insane.

Eddie It doesn't do *me* much good.

Angus What?

Eddie I said you're not made of wood. You're—flesh—and—blood—and —sporran.

Angus Aye. Well—anyway—she's away to her mother's for the week-end—which gives me plenty of time to get fit.

Angus puffs his chest and does a few "exercises". Eddie is aghast

So if you'll just show me to my room . . .

The Treatment Rooms door opens and Minnie gropes blindly in. She holds the huge spanner. She taps her way over to a radiator and prepares to hammer it

Eddie hardly sees her, but Angus is astonished

Who's *that*?

Eddie (*flatly*) That? . . . Oh—that's Minnie. (*With a sudden idea*) Minnie. Our masseuse. (*To Minnie*) You're a wonderful masseuse, aren't you, Minnie?

Minnie gropes blindly around, waving the spanner

Minnie Oh, I am, sir, I am.

Eddie (*to Angus*) Why don't you have a massage—we always start with a massage.

Angus (*horrified*) A *massage*. (*He remembers his role*) Aye—a *massage*.

Eddie Minnie—take this gentleman through and give him a massage.

Minnie (*delirious*) Oh, sir—oh, sir—where is he, sir? Point me at him . . . (*She gropes about*)

Eddie helps her to find Angus then leads them towards the Treatment Rooms door

Eddie I'll take the spanner, Minnie—and don't rush it—take your time— a really thorough massage.

Minnie Oh, sir—oh, sir—you've made me so happy—at last I've got a *real* one.

Minnie finally manages to exit to the Treatment Rooms with the bewildered Angus. Nancy appears at the window

Nancy Have you got a camera?
Eddie Outside in my car—why?
Nancy I was wondering if I could take a photograph of your little gazebo?
Eddie (*with hysterical abandon*) Why not? Everybody *else* does . . .

Eddie exits quickly through the Staff Rooms door. Nancy moves away from the window.
Mrs Court-Bending enters from the main doors, carrying Joan's suitcase

Mrs Court-Bending I say! They still haven't found that shameless wench, y'know. Disgustin' goings-on. (*She realizes the place is empty, so calls generally*) I've brought your jolly case back. (*She notices Butcher's clothing on the chair*) Oh, I say! It is my lucky day! (*She scoops up the clothing and calls generally*) Got to dash—the Millingtons are expecting me—cheeroh!

Mrs Court-Bending exits through the main doors.
Joan, in her robe, comes out of her room and downstairs, as Mr Butcher, suffering from sauna heat, staggers out of the Treatment Rooms

Joan Have you seen Edward?
Mr Butcher I'm looking for him, believe me, I'm looking for him.
Joan I understand you want to lay your hands on him.
Mr Butcher You're dead right, lady. (*A thought*) 'Ere—are you in the club?
Joan No—it's this robe. Do you know, Mr Butcher, I'm fascinated by people who do what *you* do.
Mr Butcher It 'as a certain romantic appeal, I must admit.
Joan Do you do it often?
Mr Butcher Let me put it this way—yes.
Joan Does it do any good?
Mr Butcher I've not had no complaints.
Joan They must have great faith in you.
Mr Butcher Lady, I've seen 'em pray.
Joan What exactly *is* Edward suffering from?
Mr Butcher I haven't made up my mind yet—but whatever it is, it's fatal.
Joan Good God! I hope you can do something for him.
Butcher Oh, I can, lady, I can.
Joan Just a minute—why are you wearing a gun?
Butcher What *else* can you wear with a black 'at?

Mr Butcher staggers back into the Treatment Rooms

Joan scratches her head

> *Brian enters from Room 4 carrying Nancy's clothing and Eddie's suit.*
> *He leans over the balcony*

Brian (*in a whisper*) Edward—I've got Nancy's clothes. (*Too late, he sees Joan*)
Joan *What* did you say?
Brian I said—ah! My sweet English Rose. (*He remembers he is supposed to be ill, coughs, and comes downstairs*)
Joan You were quick.
Brian Was I?
Joan You only telephoned five minutes ago.
Brian From the station. Your clothes.

He holds out the bundle. Joan takes it and he waits, fearing the worst

Joan Just a minute . . .
Brian I can explain . . .
Joan That suit is falling off you.

Brian looks down at the suit he is wearing

Brian Is it?
Joan You must have lost at least a stone. I didn't realize you were so ill—oh, my poor darling! (*She embraces and kisses him*) And to think I never noticed it before. How selfish I am—forgive me, darling.
Brian Oh, I do—I do . . .
Joan I'll be very frank, darling: I've not been satisfied with you for a long time.
Brian I know, my sweet: it's just that I get so tired I can't raise the effort.
Joan Those iron jelloids didn't do any good.
Brian To be perfectly honest, I had another look at the bottle—and according to the instructions, I should have *swallowed* them.
Joan Well, what did you *do* with them?
Brian I let them melt under my tongue.
Joan Thank God for that. I should have seen how ill you were. What can I do to make amends?
Brian Do? You can—you can—you can take some of the worry off my mind by going up to your room and resting.
Joan How can I rest? I see it even more clearly now—my place is *with you.*
Brian It isn't.
Joan It is.
Brian It isn't.
Joan Don't argue with *me*—I'm telling you it *is.* Stay here while I get dressed.

> *Joan relieves him of the bundle of clothing and goes into Room 1.*
> *Eddie dashes in from the Staff Rooms*

Eddie (*pointing desperately*) She's coming in!

Brian seems frozen to the ground. Eddie opens the cupboard door

Get your clothes off!

Brian scuttles into the cupboard. Eddie slides the door home, then moves quickly back to the Staff Rooms door just as it opens and Nancy enters from the Staff Rooms, naked, but holding the oil painting

Nancy Look what *I've* found.

She struggles through the doors. Eddie helps her and—in doing so—keeps her concealed behind the painting

It's all right—it's not very heavy.

They are staggering into the hallway, facing each other across the painting, Eddie keeping his back to the audience

Eddie No—you see—it's for my practice.
Nancy Practice—what practice?
Eddie My—dancing practice.
Nancy I never knew you danced.
Eddie Never stop. (*He cuts a little jig*)
Nancy Will you join me?
Eddie What in?
Nancy How about a tango?

There is a sudden burst of gypsy music—a band playing a tango. Eddie and Nancy begin to dance, the painting held between them. Eddie is desperately trying to stop Nancy revealing her all. Nancy, on the other hand, dances with abandon

Maxie appears from an upstairs room. He is dressed as a gypsy violinist, and mimes to the music on his violin

As the music ends, Eddie and Nancy hold a dramatic pose

Maxie exits to a bedroom. The cupboard door opens to show Brian naked, but concealed behind Minnie's suitcase. He steps out, with arms raised, just as the music ends

Brian Olé!

Eddie and Nancy turn to see him

(*Brightly*) Ah, there you are. Having fun, see.
Nancy (*indicating the suitcase*) You're not leaving, are you?
Brian I've only just arrived—that is—no.
Nancy Why are you carrying a suitcase?
Brian I found it. At the bottom of the swimming pool.

Nancy I've been looking for you everywhere.

Brian I was in the cupboard. Looking for some polish. To polish my suitcase.

*Suddenly there is a great bellow of rage, unidentifiable—it might come
from a moose*

Nancy My husband!

Another bellow

If he sees me like this, he'll go mad!

Another bellow

Brian He already *has*.

Nancy He mustn't find me here.

*Nancy looks around, sees the open cupboard door and—under cover of
the painting held by Eddie—goes into the cupboard*

Eddie and Brian breathe sighs of relief

Brian (*almost immediately*) What about *me*?

*Eddie hands him the painting and Brian "hides" behind it whilst still covering
his dignity with the suitcase*

*The Treatment Rooms door bursts open and Angus comes out—wearing
only a towel round his waist. His neck is cricked so that his head is at an
angle. He is followed by Minnie who can only twitter tearfully. She wears
motor-cycle goggles and rubber gloves*

*Brian is pressed against the rear wall, out of Angus's eyeline as he comes in.
Throughout the following, Brian contrives to stand, with his suitcase, behind
Angus. Angus suspects that someone is behind him, but because of the painful
movement of his neck, is never quite able to turn round and see*

Eddie Oh, Angus—how are you?

Angus How am I? I'm in agony, that's how I am.

Eddie What's happened?

Angus What's *happened*? *Look* at me.

Eddie (*indicating the towel*) You've changed your kilt.

Angus *This*. (*He points to his bent head*)

Eddie What have you *done*, Minnie?

Minnie Oh, sir, all I did was touch it and it popped clean out of its socket.

*Minnie bursts into tears and gropes her way back into the Treatment
Rooms*

Angus Don't just stand there, man, *do* something.

Eddie Do something—yes, of course—do something.

The Staff Rooms door bursts open and Maxie enters. He is done up as an Indian doctor—white coat, turban, and is adorned with clusters of medical equipment, stethoscopes, etc

Maxie Stand aside, please.
Angus Who are you?
Maxi Doctor Gunghi Singh.
Eddie Our resident physiotherapist.
Maxie Quite so. (*He snaps a finger*) A chair, if you please.

Eddie brings a chair. Maxie seats Angus, then takes out an ordinary household torch

Say "Ah".
Angus Ahrrrr . . .

Maxie shines the torch into Angus's ear

Eddie Why does a Scotsman always roll his Ahrr's?
Maxie To make his kilt swing.

Maxie takes out a small hammer and taps Angus's pain-racked head. Angus bellows

There's only one answer.

Brian lowers the painting to reveal his face

Eddie } Yes? { *Speaking*
Brian } { *together*

Brian covers up again with the painting

Maxie Cut his head off and start again.

The Treatment Rooms door bursts open and Mr Butcher staggers in. He is practically overcome by the sauna heat

Mr Butcher Some rotter's stolen my best suit!
Eddie Is *nothing* sacred?

All eyes have turned to Mr Butcher—apart from the anguished Angus

Mr Butcher (*points to Angus*) Where's 'e come from?
Eddie Scotland. *Yard. Scotland Yard.* (*Hissing*) Remember The Great Train Robbers?
Mr Butcher You don't mean 'e arrested 'em?
Eddie No—but he *would* have done if his kilt hadn't been at the cleaners.
Mr Butcher They're closing in!
Eddie You're right! Stay in the sauna until the heat's off!

Mr Butcher staggers back into the Treatment Rooms

(*Pleasantly*) Where *were* we?

Angus My *head*!

Brian lowers the painting to reveal his face

Brian Couldn't you try some manipulation? (*He covers up again with the painting*)

Maxie Good idea. I think I've got a bottle in my bag.

Eddie Manipulation—(*he mimes kneading fingers*)—under the heat lamp. (*He indicates Maxie to get Angus out to the Treatment Rooms*)

Maxie We can try. This way, if you please.

Maxie takes Angus's arm and guides him towards the Treatment Rooms door

Angus (*as they go*) You're quite sure you know what you're doing?

Maxie Most indubitably.

Angus How long have you been practising?

Maxie Ever since I was a lad: but I'm getting better.

Maxie and Angus exit to the Treatment Rooms

Eddie and Brian heave sighs of relief

Brian (*remembering*) Nancy . . . (*He backs towards the cupboard—still concealed behind the suitcase*)

Joan enters from Room 1

Joan (*angrily*) Where is my husband?

At the sound of her voice, Brian panics and gets into the cupboard, closing the door

Joan comes downstairs, closing the window. She is wearing Nancy's clothing. Eddie still holds the painting

Joan Where is he?

Eddie Something wrong?

Joan Look at these clothes.

Eddie Very attractive.

Joan They're not *mine*.

Eddie Ah *yes*—now he said something about that.

Joan *What?*

Eddie He borrowed them. From his secretary.

Unseen by Joan, Minnie enters from the Treatment Rooms. She is carrying a pile of towels. She gropes across towards the cupboard, opens the cupboard door, Brian takes the towels, Minnie closes the door and exits to the Treatment Rooms

Joan (*during this*) His secretary is sixty-three years old.

Eddie But young in heart.

Joan Where *is* he?
Eddie In the garden.

Joan glares at Eddie suspiciously, then exits through the Staff Rooms door

Eddie waits a moment, then goes to open the cupboard door slightly

All clear.

Brian comes out, wrapped in one of the towels. Nancy puts her head round the door, then comes out. She is also wrapped in one of the towels

Nancy Where's Angus?
Eddie Having his head examined.
Brian I think I'll join him.
Eddie Nancy—go to your room—get dressed—we'll think of something.

Nancy moves to the stairs and mounts them

Nancy I was *so* enjoying myself.

Nancy exits to Room 3

Eddie Right. We've got to get her out of here. As soon as she's dressed, you can drive her to the station.
Brian Yes. I'll wait in the car. (*He moves to the main doors, then stops*) I can't go like *this*.
Eddie Why not?
Brian My *clothes*.
Eddie Put them on then.
Brian I haven't *got* any!

Nancy appears at her door

Nancy They've gone!
Brian Who?
Nancy My clothes!
Eddie (*remembering*) Joan.
Brian What have we *done*?
Nancy What can I *do*?
Eddie Stay in your room.
Nancy I can't!
Eddie You must!

Nancy exits to Room 3. As she does, Minnie enters from the Treatment Rooms, groping her way towards the Staff Rooms door

Eddie Minnie.

Minnie turns and gropes back blindly towards him

Minnie Yes, sir—yes, sir . . .

Eddie (*to Brian*) I've had an idea.

Brian Not another one—I can't stand it.

Eddie (*to Minnie*) I'm giving you one more chance, Minnie.

Minnie Oh, sir—oh, sir—anything, sir—*anything*.

Eddie Yes, all right, Minnie—now listen carefully—the lady in Room
Three——

Minnie —Room Three——

Eddie —she wants a mud-pack.

Minnie (*ecstatic*) Oh, sir!

Brian You're not turning her loose on someone *else*?

Eddie She can't leave here until we get her clothes back—so for the time
being, she'll have to stay—and we daren't risk him seeing her. (*To
Minnie*) Minnie, my fate is in your hands. I'm depending on you. Now
tell me what you've got to do.

Minnie I'm to give him a mud-pack.

Eddie *Her* a mud-pack.

Minnie Her—yes—her.

Eddie Who?

Minnie Lady Groomtree.

Eddie The lady in Room Three.

Minnie Yes—the lady in Room Three.

Eddie As quickly as you can.

Minnie (*excitedly*) As quick as I can—Room Three—quick as I can—
Room Three . . .

Minnie exits to the Treatment Rooms

Eddie moves to the Staff Room door

Brian Where are you going?

Eddie To keep your wife out of the way.

*Eddie exits. Brian exits to Room 4. Minnie enters from the Treatment
Rooms carrying a large bucket, ladles and spoons. She stumbles up the
the stairs*

Minnie As quick as I can—Room Three—quick as I can—Room Three . . .

*Minnie is half-way up the stairs when Mrs Court-Bending enters through
the main doors, carrying Joan's suitcase*

Mrs Court-Bending I say! They're still playing about in your bushes!

*Minnie is still hurrying upstairs repeating her instructions. She goes into
Room 4 and is ushered out and into Room 3 by Brian*

Anything else for me, is there? (*Indicating the case*) The Millingtons
just gave me some wonderful toys for the kiddies . . .

By now Brian has got Minnie into Room 3. He leans over the balcony

Brian (*desperately*) They're not up here, they're in the cupboard.
Mrs Court-Bending What are?
Brian The clothes.

Brian suddenly realizes that he is half-naked and talking to a complete stranger. He exits quickly to Room 4

Mrs Court-Bending In the cupboard, are they? (*She moves to the cupboard*) Not to worry—I can look after m'self. (*She opens the cupboard, looks inside, and pulls out Eddie's suit*) I say—jolly good.

Mrs Court-Bending puts the case down, opens it, and takes out some toys to stuff the clothes in

Mr Butcher staggers in from the Treatment Rooms, brandishing his gun

Mr Butcher Eddie—I'm gonna give it to yer.
Mrs Court-Bending Thanks awfully. (*She takes the gun from the dumbstruck Mr Butcher and puts it in the case*)
Mr Butcher That's a real gun!
Mrs Court-Bending Of *course* it is, you naughty boy, you . . . (*She takes up a toy sub-machine-gun and turns it on him with*) They *all* are! Rat-tat-tat!

Mr Butcher throws up his hands and presses back against the door

Mr Butcher Who sent you?
Mrs Court-Bending The local organization.
Butcher How big is it?
Mrs Court-Bending World-wide, dear boy—world-wide! (*She is packing everything into the case*)
Mr Butcher I'm from the London organization myself.
Mrs Court-Bending Oh, yes? I know your top man.
Mr Butcher (*confidingly*) The police are 'ere.
Mrs Court-Bending Of course—*I* sent for them.
Mr Butcher Don't tell me you've got a tie-up with the law?
Mrs Court-Bending A tie-up? I'd go so far as to say that I've got the Chief Constable eating out of my hand.
Mr Butcher A bent copper!
Mrs Court-Bending Nonsense! We've got three fine boys and a horse called Paddy.
Mr Butcher Paddy the 'Orse! I thought he was inside.
Mrs Court-Bending Only during the winter. (*Confidentially*) Actually, he's having a lot of trouble with his fetlocks.
Mr Butcher I keep telling 'im to change his tailor.
Mrs Court-Bending Oh well—can't stop—enjoyed our chat—you know—whoever you are—you've made someone—somewhere—jolly happy.

Mrs Court-Bending exits quickly through the main doors

Mr Butcher I don't care what you say—this place ain't 'ealthy.

Mr Butcher staggers back into the Treatment Rooms.
  Silence. Then the door to Room 4 slowly opens and Brian comes out.
He is "wearing" a Marks and Spencers' shopping bag as a pair of shorts.
He comes cautiously downstairs when Eddie enters from the Staff Rooms.

Brian closes the window, turns, and jumps at seeing Eddie. Eddie can only
stare at Brian's appearance

Brian (*shivering*) Well?
Eddie I told her you were having a rest.
Brian How can I *rest*? *Look* at me.
Eddie I'd rather not . . . (*Pulling himself together*) Everything's under
    control—Joan's in the garden—Angus is in the heat room—Nancy's
    getting a mud-pack.
Brian That's wonderful—everything's under control except my body.
    Look at it. Not only am I frightened to death, I'm *freezing* to death.
    (*His whole body is shaking*)
Eddie Put some clothes on then.
Brian I was just going to when that *woman* appeared.
Eddie What woman?
Brian I don't *know*. I don't *care*—I want my clothes—your clothes—
    anybody's clothes! (*He opens the cupboard and looks in*) They've gone!
Eddie They can't have.
Brian They've gone!

Eddie looks into the cupboard

Joan Is anyone there?
Brian ⎱ No! ⎰ *Speaking*
Eddie ⎰   ⎱ *together*

Brian goes into the cupboard, closing the door. Eddie exits to the Treat-
ment Rooms. Joan enters from the Staff Rooms

Joan Brian? Eddie? (*She moves to the stairs*) I could have sworn I heard
    someone here . . .

There is a sudden loud sneeze

    Bless you.
Brian (*in the cupboard*) Thank you, my sweet.
Joan My pleasure. (*A few more steps and she realizes. She returns to fling*
    open the cupboard door)

Brian is sitting in the wheelchair in his paper bag. He's shivering like mad

    What are you doing in that cupboard?

Brian There's a perfectly reasonable explanation, but I'm afraid you might find it boring.

Joan I'm waiting.

Brian So am I.

Joan *What for?*

Brian What for? (*With a sudden idea*) The thief!

Joan What thief?

Brian The thief who stole my clothes. Yes—that's it—the thief. I'm lying in wait for him.

Joan Are you trying to tell me there's a thief at large?

Eddie enters from the Treatment Rooms with Angus's kilt

Brian Why else do you think I'm sitting in this cupboard with no clothes on?

Eddie Exactly.

Joan He must have taken my suitcase.

Eddie Of course. And your dress. We've been trying to keep it from you so that you wouldn't worry.

Joan And that's why all those policemen are running about outside?

Eddie } *Of course!* { *Speaking*
Brian } { *together*

Joan What will you do if he comes back?

Eddie Yes—what will you do?

Brian Do? I'll call the police.

Joan From in *there*?

Brian With my whistle.

Joan What whistle?

Brian No—not my whistle—my trumpet. (*He produces the ear trumpet and blows a feeble note on it*)

Joan It's not very loud.

Eddie Well, we don't want to scare him off. (*To Brian*) Put this on—it's all I could find. (*He tosses the kilt at Brian and closes the cupboard door*)

Joan He could be violent.

Eddie Brian? *Never*.

Joan The *thief*.

Eddie Brian will take care of him.

Joan I never knew he was so brave.

Eddie There's a lot of things you don't know about him—thank God.

Joan You can't just leave him *sitting* there.

Eddie takes her arm

Eddie (*sincerely*) It's the only way.

Joan But he's got no clothes on. He's *ill*.

Eddie You're right. I'll get some.

Joan looks round and starts for the stairs

Minnie comes out of Room 3. She is having one of her breakdowns. She stumbles, sobbing, down the stairs and exits to the Staff Rooms.

Nancy appears at the door of Room 3. She is wearing her robe, has her hair in a towel turban, and her face is a black mess

Joan can only stare as Nancy comes downstairs so that they are face to face. The mud-pack on Nancy's face has set so hard that she cannot speak. She waves her arms frantically—pointing to her face

Eddie enters quickly from the Treatment Rooms

Nancy—seeing him—tries to mime that she cannot speak

Joan What's wrong with her?

Eddie Wrong? What makes you think something's wrong?

Joan The way she's waving her arms about.

Eddie Oh, that. That's just her exercises—that's why she comes here— for the exercise. (*To Nancy*) Up—one, two—up—one, two . . . (*He waves his arms about—trying to copy the frantic movements made by Nancy*)

Joan Why doesn't she speak?

Eddie She *does*. Only not our language. (*Intimately, to Joan*) Foreign, you know.

Nancy suddenly stops moving and stares at Joan. Joan is quite worried as Nancy advances on her. She points to the clothes Joan is wearing. She mimes "those are mine!"

Isn't it amazing how these foreigners all love English clothes?

Joan What's she trying to say?

Eddie I think she wants to know where you bought them. (*To Nancy*) Marks and Sparks, I should think, dear.

Joan I wouldn't know. They're not mine.

Nancy frantically mimes: "No—they're mine" and tries to get the clothes off Joan

Unhand me, madam!

Eddie (*intervening*) Yes—unhand her, madam!

Joan (*freeing herself*) Outrageous!

Eddie Appalling!

Eddie tries to placate Nancy behind Joan's back. Nancy sinks miserably into a chair

Joan I shall go to my room.

Eddie Yes, *I* should.

Joan climbs the stairs haughtily

Joan And they seriously expect us to stay in the Common Market? Over my dead body.

Eddie I couldn't agree with you more.

Joan exits to Room 1, slamming the door

Eddie immediately moves over to Nancy. She mimes "look at my face". Eddie examines it, taps her cheek with his knuckles

It's like a brick.

Nancy's shoulders begin to heave as she begins to weep. Eddie puts his arms around her and lifts her from the chair

There, there, there . . . *I'll* see to it. (*He guides her into the Treatment Room*) We'll soon have that lump off your head—I mean, weight off your mind . . .

Eddie and Nancy exit. A moment later, Minnie stumbles on from the Staff Rooms

Minnie Everything I do goes wrong! It was never like this with Phillip . . .

Minnie opens the cupboard door. Brian sits in the chair. Minnie drags out the wheelchair

I must keep practising—all I did was get hold of his head . . . (*She grasps Brian's head*)

Angus enters from the Treatment Rooms, still in towel with cricked neck

Angus It'd doing no good, I'm telling you! (*Seeing Minnie*) Stay away from me, woman!

Minnie shrieks

(*Seeing Brian*) Who's this poor devil you're destroying?
Minnie He's not a devil, he's my Phillip and he likes it—look—he *likes* it. (*She begins to massage furiously at Brian who remains in silent agony, bending his limbs at her will*)

Maxie—as the physiotherapist—enters from the Treatment Rooms with a glass of water

Maxie (*to Angus*) Drink this.

Angus takes the glass and tosses the water over his shoulder—where his head would normally be

Feel better?
Angus There's a strange tickling down my spine.
Maxie Good—it's beginning to work. (*He guides Angus towards the Treatment Rooms*) Back to the heat.
Angus I can't stand it!
Maxie Lie down then.

Angus and Maxie exit to the Treatment Rooms. Eddie enters from the Gymnasium

Brian leaps up from the chair, to show that he now wears the wig and the kilt. He has one arm wedged down inside the kilt

Brian I've had enough.

Minnie screams

Minnie He's alive—he's alive. Phillip—Phillip . . .

Minnie bodily picks up Brian and carries him across stage. He pulls himself free, so that he collapses to the floor. He jumps to his feet

Brian I am not your dummy, madam! (*He moves quickly to the cupboard to drag out the sorbo dummy—now naked and bald*) This is your Phillip and I am personally going to strangle him—d'you hear? *Strangle* him. (*He seizes the dummy by the throat and with a maniacal laugh begins to strangle it. The dummy's head bends over at an angle*)

Minnie screams and wrestles the dummy from his grip. She stares at him in a moment of impotent rage

Minnie You—you—snake in the grass!
Brian I, madam, am a chartered accountant.
Minnie All right! You—you—adder!

Minnie exits quickly through the main doors

Brian (*almost at breakdown point*) I'm innocent . . . you understand? Innocent . . . (*To God*) *You* believe me, don't you? *You* believe me . . . (*He breaks down*)
Eddie Pull yourself together. Just remember . . . you're a chartered accountant.
Brian You're right. (*He pulls himself together*)
Eddie I'll have to take that kilt.
Brian You can't—it's mine—it's mine . . . ! (*He grasps the kilt possessively*)
Eddie It's Angus's—and he'll be wanting it.

They grapple for the kilt near the window. Brian opens it and tries to climb out. Eddie restrains him by the kilt

Brian He can't have it—possession is nine parts of the law.
Eddie *English* law.
Brian We're *in* England.
Eddie But it's a Scotch kilt.
Brian Scot*tish*.
Eddie All right—sort of Scotch. And Scotch law is different.
Brian How?
Eddie In Scotland they say: "It's a braw bracht moonlicht kilt that you canna wear when another mon's got his head in a timorous wee sling, d'yer ken?"

Brian Do they really?

Eddie And there's a fine of five hundred pounds—so get it off.

Brian What can I put on?

Eddie I dunno! No—wait a minute—Maxie's got a trunkful of stuff up-stairs—you're bound to find something.

Brian hurries upstairs

Brian Which room?

Eddie Number Two.

Brian stops outside Room 2, does a little jiggle, and then tosses the kilt over the gallery to the waiting Eddie

Brian exits to Room 2. Joan enters from Room 1

Joan Where's that insane foreigner?

Eddie Having his head put right.

Joan Him? I thought it was a woman?

Eddie Oh—*that* foreigner. Looking for you.

Joan (*worried*) Where?

Eddie I told her you were in the garden. Stay in your room.

Joan exits to Room 1. Eddie looks down at the kilt he is holding, has a thought, and exits quickly to the Staff Rooms.
    The stage is empty for a moment. Then Minnie stumbles in through the main doors, dragging the cricked-necked dummy. At the same time, we hear the sound of approaching police whistles

Minnie If only my passionate pirate would come and take us away from all this!

Minnie drags the dummy through into the Staff Rooms. The Sergeant enters from the main doors. He blows his whistle

Sergeant Nobody move! (*He looks round the empty hallway and moves across*)

Joan enters from Room 1

Joan (*seeing the Sergeant*) Officer!

The Sergeant jumps

Sergeant If you don't mind—I almost swallowed my whistle. I'll have a word with you, madam, if I may.

Joan Of course.

The Sergeant, pulling out his notebook, as she comes downstairs, closing the window

Sergeant I take it you know what's going on?

Joan I do and it's disgusting—people running about with no clothes.

Sergeant There's been a development.

Joan You've made an arrest.

Sergeant An arrest, I dare say, is imminent. Only we now have reason to believe there are two more of 'em.

Joan *Two*. How frightening.

Sergeant A frightening sight indeed, madam. Yes. I was leaning against a tree, having a quiet fag—that's police jargon for maintaining a vigilant look-out—when I perceived two figures moving away from this building at what I can only describe as breakneck speed.

Joan They must have been disturbed.

Sergeant Very disturbed by the look of 'em.

Joan I expect it was my husband.

Sergeant Is this by way of being a confession, madam?

Joan Confession?

Sergeant You say your husband was in the garden.

Joan No—in the cupboard. With his trumpet.

Sergeant (*looking at her askance*) Let me get this quite clear. Your husband is in a cupboard. With a trumpet.

Joan Yes.

Sergeant Some sort of concert, is it?

Joan Would you like to speak to him?

Sergeant Yes, and no. That is—later. Now, if you don't mind, madam . . . (*He clears his throat and refers to his notebook*) Here is an official description of the persons for whom we are looking for. A short, lumpy lady and a tall dark, loose-limbed man, carrying his head at an unusual angle—caused, I suspect, by looking through too many keyholes—last seen leaping across the lawn with cries of "Oh, my Phillip; oh, my Prince!" (*He shuts his notebook*) No doubt they'll be linking up with the other hussy somewhere in the bushes.

Joan What would they be doing in the bushes?

Sergeant Practising their fearful rites, if you ask me. Smoking lumps of pottery, making human sacrifices—stuff like that. Seems a very popular area for that sort of thing.

Joan It's happened before?

Sergeant There was a case of it last year: all these elderly gentlemen dancing round great chunks of rock, pretending to be *witches*.

Joan It sounds like a lot of old warlocks.

Sergeant Precisely *my* attitude, madam. Mind you, after this they'll be after me for me memoirs—Black Magic On My Beat—A Country Copper Tells All, price thirty pence.

Joan What shall I do if I see them?

Sergeant I'd buy a copy if I was you, madam—a very descriptive style I've got, though I say it myself.

Joan I meant the three criminals.

Sergeant Cover your eyes and dial nine-nine-nine.

Joan Shouldn't I tell my husband to blow his trumpet?

Sergeant If he feels it coming over him—by all means tell him to give it a blow. Never keep it in if it's bursting to come out, that's what I always say. (*He moves towards the main doors*) Have no fear, madam: we shall keep an ever watchful eye on the premises. You can sleep easy tonight.

The Sergeant blows his whistle and exits through the main doors. Eddie— unseen by Joan—puts his head round the Staff Rooms door. He is about to enter, when Angus enters from the Treatment Rooms, still in the towel with cricked neck. Eddie goes to Room 1 without being seen and exits

Angus Where's my kilt?

Joan Angus!

Angus (*in a mixture of complete surprise and quiet*) Joan. I never knew *you* were here.

Joan I didn't know you were here.

Angus I've only just arrived—and *look* at me.

Joan Have you been sent for some treatment?

Angus (*in a rage*) Have I been . . . ! (*Remembering*) Aye—that's right— my doctor said they should have a look at it.

Joan And have they looked at it?

Angus *Looked* at it—they've been *trampling* on it.

Joan Well, at least it must give you a different outlook on life.

Angus Tell me, Joan, are you here on your own?

Joan Oh, no, I'm with Brian.

Angus (*guiltily*) Brian! Where is he?

Joan (*suddenly remembering, speaking softly*) Waiting for the thief.

Angus What thief?

She motions for him to whisper

Joan The thief who took your kilt. Would you like a quick word with him? (*She moves to the cupboard*)

Angus No, no, no—not if he's busy . . .

Joan Better tell him it's us or he'll blow his trumpet—and we don't want that, do we?

Angus (*bewildered*) Oh, no, we don't want that.

Joan taps on the cupboard door

Joan Brian, don't blow your trumpet, it's me—Joan. (*She waits, then opens the door slightly, then slides it fully open*) He's not there. He must have found a clue. Yes. He's hunting down the criminal—all alone. *Criminals*. Three of them. (*Turning to Angus*) You must find him— help him.

Angus (*backing away*) I'd rather he didn't know that I'm—that is—better he does whatever he's doing on his own.

Joan You coward!

Angus (*in full pomp*) If a man's got to do what a man's got to do, it's better that he does it the way he do it, and better to have done it on his own than never to have done it at all. (*He sits*) Aye.

Joan Don't you realize what sort of man he is? Who else would face those three monsters armed with nothing but a suitcase and a trumpet. Who else would drag themselves off a sickbed and go racing back to London just because *you* asked him to?

Angus I haven't spoken to him for nearly a week.

Joan My hero—my wonderful misunderst... (*She stops, realizes*) Do you mean to say he didn't go to London to see you?

Angus Of course he didn't—I've been trying to avoid him for a—I mean —*no*.

Joan Then why did he say he *did*? (*Referring to her clothes*) And where did he get these clothes?

Angus Oh, those—they're Nancy's. She was wearing them when she went to see her mother.

There is a pause

Joan }Nancy! { *Speaking*
Angus }   { *together*

Joan moves around, working herself into a cold rage. Angus, totally bewildered still, moves around scratching where his head would normally be

Joan So that's why he's been avoiding me—that's why he's been trying to keep me out of the way—and all the time he's been with—with— (*she pulls at the dress she wears*)—this woman! *Your wife!*

Angus You mean they're *here—together*?

Joan We must find them—and expose them.

Angus Is that really necessary?

Joan What sort of man *are* you?

Angus (*his pomp rising*) I know what I am, woman. If a man's got to do what a man's got to do ...

Joan (*covering her ears*) Oh, don't start all *that* again. (*She thinks a moment*) Did she take any other clothes?

Angus No.

Joan (*referring to the dress*) Then this is all she has.

Angus So?

Joan So she'll be walking about in the——

Angus —in the hope of finding them.

Joan And *he'll* be helping her. The swine. We'll set a trap—using these clothes as bait. (*Looking around*) There isn't much time. (*Going to the cupboard*) I'll do it in here—then as soon as they make a move, we can pounce.

Angus I'm not too good at pouncing.

Joan (*in the cupboard*) I'll hand the clothes out to you—put them on the desk—where they can see them—then hide yourself.

She is about to slide the door shut but has another thought

How will I know when they come?

Angus I'll—give you a signal.

Joan What signal?

Angus I'll whistle—"Rule Britannia".

Joan nods and slides the door shut

Angus puts one hand over his eyes and extends the other hand ready to receive the clothing, standing like the statue of The Thinker

The door of Room 2 slowly opens and Brian sticks his head out before moving to the top of the stairs. He is dressed as a pirate, in a bare-armed shirt, three-cornered hat, leather jerkin, on the shoulder of which lolls a stuffed parrot, carries a large cutlass, and hobbles on a wooden leg fashioned from a sink plunger

Brian tries to get down the stairs on the wooden leg—using a broomstick for support, but gives up and walks down, so that the wooden leg sticks out horizontally above his knee. Suddenly he sees Angus and freezes. Both men are stock still. Then, slowly, Angus lowers the hand that covers his eyes. The two men stare at each other; give feeble grins. Brian opens the window and looks out, hand to brow, sailor fashion, then moves to the desk, picks up a pencil, sharpens it with his cutlass, studiously examining the pencil and avoiding Angus. Satisfied, he puts the pencil back on the desk and rams the cutlass back into his belt. But this time the cutlass goes down inside his trouser leg. Brian almost collapses but recovers and turns to face Angus

Brian Is that *you*, Angus?
Angus (*looking at himself*) Aye—so it is.
Brian (*very casually*) Staying long?
Angus No, no. Just passing through.
Brian Well, there's a coincidence—so am I.
Angus Well, I won't detain you.
Brian Got to be going myself.
Angus Well—well—there's a coincidence.
Brian See you back in London then.
Angus Aye, see you back in London.

Both men linger. Brian casually starts to whistle "Rule Britannia" as he exits backwards through the Gymnasium door, and Angus exits backwards through the Treatment Rooms door. They wave to each other as they go

When Brian and Angus are out of sight the cupboard door slides partly open and Joan's hand waves

Joan (*inside the cupboard*) Not yet, Angus—my zip's stuck!

The cupboard door slides shut

For a moment the stage is empty. Then Angus and Brian creep simultaneously back through the Gymnasium and Treatment Rooms doors, backs to each other, when the cutlass in Brian's belt makes contact with Angus's behind and they both jump, grin guiltily and wave a friendly greeting

Throughout the following, Brian moves to stand directly in front of the cupboard door

Angus Just missed my train.

Brian So did I—that is—just missed my boat.

Angus Oh, you're going sailing, are you?

Brian Yes, yes—away on the evening tide.

Angus It's a great life, so they say.

Brian Yes, yes—a great life. You—er—you didn't want to have a little chat about anything, did you, Angus?

Angus No, no—just passing through.

Brian Well, well—there's a coincidence. (*By now he is against the cupboard door, and in his attempt to look casual, puts both arms behind his back, and crosses his legs. This proves somewhat difficult in view of the dangling wooden leg*)

The cupboard door opens slightly and Joan's arm comes out, holding an item of underwear. Since Brian is directly in front of the cupboard, the arm goes underneath one of his arms, so that the effect is of Brian holding out the underwear. He looks down at it aghast, then up at Angus, grinning amiably. The hand begins to wave the underwear impatiently

I expect you're wondering what I'm doing?

Angus (*generously*) No, no . . .

Brian It's what we seamen call semaphore—sending messages—S O S.

The hand drops the garment, withdraws, drops two more. Brian follows its progress. The hand makes the thumbs-up sign. Brian makes the thumbs-up sign with both his hands—so that there are three hands in a row. Joan's hand withdraws, the cupboard closes. Brian grins amiably at Angus

Well, mustn't keep the Admiral waiting . . .

Brian steps over the pile of clothing—then walks slowly, and with what he believes to be dignity, to the stairs. He tries to maintain the dignity whilst manœuvring the wooden leg up the stairs. He fails, and, grasping the leg, stumbles up the stairs and into Room 2, slamming the door after him

Angus stares up the stairs, then moves forward to take up the clothes

Mrs Court-Bending enters through the main doors carrying Joan's suitcase in one hand, and Mr Butcher's gun in the other

Mrs Court-Bending Hello there!

Angus stares at her

Those for *me*?

Angus remains frozen as she puts her case on a chair, opens it, and takes the clothing from him

Romp. *

Every time I bring the jolly old case back, I get another bundle. Be needing the jolly old trailer next, what? (*She thrusts the clothing into the case, locks it, shakes Angus's unwilling hand*) Jolly nice meeting you. Mr Manchip about, is he? Got something I think I ought to tell him. Just a tickey though—don't I know you? Don't I recognize you from somewhere? (*She cocks her head to look him straight in the eye*) I could have sworn I . . . (*Suddenly she realizes and, backing away from Angus in horror, gives a cry*) It's *him*! Officer—officer—it's *him*! (*She gives an ear-piercing scream and faints away, to sprawl in a chair*)

Angus comes to life and dashes over to her

Angus Control yourself, woman—have you never seen a Scotsman without his kilt before?

Mrs Court-Bending opens her eyes momentarily, sees Angus, screams, and faints away. As his gun hand goes up in the air the gun explodes with a roar. Angus backs away from her, terrified

The Sergeant enters quickly through the main doors. He sees Angus and gives a blast on his whistle.
At the sound of the whistle, Joan puts her head round the cupboard door, sees the Sergeant, and goes back inside

The Sergeant advances on Angus, pulling out a set of handcuffs. Angus backs away

Sergeant Stop—in the name of the Law!

Angus turns and runs into the Gymnasium. The Sergeant blows his whistle and exits after nim.
Nancy enters from the Treatment Rooms, now wearing the kilt as a mini-dress. Her face is still blacked-up. She exits to the Gymnasium as Angus enters from the Treatment Rooms and hurries upstairs into Room 4.
Eddie enters from Room 1 as the Sergeant enters from the Treatment Rooms. He sees Eddie and blows his whistle. Eddie exits to Room 1.
The Sergeant climbs the stairs and exits to Room 1.
Eddie enters from Room 3, comes downstairs, and is about to go into the Treatment Rooms when the door swings open, concealing him behind it.
Mr Butcher staggers out from the Treatment Rooms and exits to the Gymnasium. Maxie enters from the Treatment Rooms dressed as a police constable.

Maxie Evening, all.

The Treatment Rooms door swings shut, and as it does Eddie exits through it, unseen by Maxie.
Angus enters from Room 4, sees Maxie as the policeman, and exits into Room 3.

Nancy enters from the Gymnasium. The Sergeant enters from Room 4, sees Nancy, and blows his whistle. Joan's head appears momentarily round the cupboard door. Nancy exits to the Treatment Rooms

The Sergeant comes downstairs and sees Maxie, who stands making notes in his book

Sergeant *You!* Surround the house!

Maxie salutes, pockets his notebook and exits through the main doors.
    Mr Butcher enters from the Gymnasium, sees the Sergeant, and exits to the Treatment Rooms.
    The Sergeant exits to the Treatment Rooms.
    Eddie enters from the Gymnasium, goes upstairs, and exits to Room 4.
    Brian enters from Room 2 and comes downstairs dressed as the pirate. He exits to the Staff Rooms.
    Nancy enters from the Treatment Rooms and goes upstairs to exit to Room 3.
    Mr Butcher enters from the Treatment Rooms and exits to the Gymnasium.
    Angus enters from Room 1.
    Mr Butcher enters from the Gymnasium and exits to Room 4.
    The Sergeant enters from the Gymnasium, sees Angus and mounts the stairs. Angus exits to Room 2.
    Brian dashes in from the Staff Room, hotly pursued by Minnie, and they run up the stairs

Minnie (*as they go*) It's him! It's him! My pirate has returned for his Minnie . . .

    The Sergeant exits to Room 2. Angus enters from Room 1.
    Brian exits to Room 4, hotly pursued by Minnie. Angus exits to Room 3.
    The Sergeant enters from Room 1 and exits to Room 4.
    Brian and Minnie enter from Room 2. She pursues him downstairs and into the Treatment Rooms.
    Eddie enters from Room 2, comes downstairs and exits to the Staff Rooms.
    Mr Butcher enters from Room 1 and exits to the Gymnasium.
    Nancy enters from Room 1 and exits to Room 3.
    Angus enters from Room 2 and exits to Room 4.
    The Sergeant enters from Room 1 and exits to Room 2

Doors 2, 3 and 4 close simultaneously. Silence

    Doors 2 opens and the Sergeant puts his head out. He comes cautiously out on to the gallery and starts to creep downstairs. His shoes creak loudly. He goes into a routine (using a hand squeaker) of being pursued by his own creaking shoes before dashing back into Room 2.

Angus's head peers round the Gymnasium door. All clear

Angus moves quietly to the centre of the room when, suddenly and simultaneously:

> *Door 1 opens to reveal Minnie.*
> *Door 2 opens to reveal the Sergeant.*
> *Door 3 opens to reveal Nancy.*
> *Door 4 opens to reveal Brian.*
> *Mr Butcher puts his head round the Treatment Rooms door.*
> *The Staff Rooms door opens to reveal Eddie.*
> *Maxie appears at the window as the police constable.*
> *Mrs Court-Bending stirs with a groan in the chair.*
> *Angus is seized with panic. He dashes into the cupboard, closing the door behind him*

The Sergeant blows his whistle, then moves majestically down the stairs, saluting Maxie en route

Sergeant Nice bit of house surrounding, lad. (*He closes the window on Maxie and moves across to throw open the cupboard door*)

> *Angus and Joan are revealed, both apparently naked, hiding behind one towel.*
> *Mr Butcher staggers back into the Treatment Rooms*

Mrs Court-Bending screams and faints. The Sergeant points to Joan and Angus

Sergeant You two—out of there—(*crooks a finger to Brian and Nancy*)—you two—down 'ere.

As Brian and Nancy come downstairs, Eddie enters from the Staff Rooms, Maxie disappears from the window and Minnie drifts back into Room 1

(*Throughout the above*) Now then. Serious complaints have been lodged concerning your behaviour. It is my duty to warn you that any evidence you might give will be taken down . . . on second thoughts, perhaps not.

Angus Now look here, I'm a respectable citizen . . .

Joan I've never been so humiliated in all my life . . .

Brian *You've* never been so humiliated . . .

Nancy What were you doing in that cupboard?

Eddie It all seems perfectly clear to me . . .

Joan
Nancy } Shut up! { *Speaking*
Angus   *together*
Brian

The Sergeant blows his whistle

Sergeant Any more of these interruptions and you'll *all* be in the nick. (*To Angus and Joan*) I have reason to believe that you two have been cavorting about in the undergrowth, starkers.
Joan Absolutely ridiculous.
Sergeant Nine hundred and thirty-four devoted pairs of eyes cannot lie.
Angus I haven't set foot outside this place since I arrived.

The Sergeant produces his notebook

Sergeant (*reading*) "A tall, dark, hairy man, carrying his head at an unusual angle." (*He moves to Angus, and cocks his head so that they are face to face*) I'd say that fitted you to a T, sir—so if you'll just pop along with me to the station—and you, madam.

The Sergeant indicates for them to exit at the main doors. Joan and Angus begin a bad-tempered struggle for the single towel

Joan Let me have this towel . . . !
Angus Now look here, Joan . . .

The towel rips, giving them half each

Joan My clothes were stolen, I tell you!
Sergeant A likely story.

The Sergeant laughs merrily. He looks at Eddie and Brian who join in, but trail off under the wilting glare of Angus and Joan

Angus It's perfectly true.
Sergeant I see. So, what you are saying is that you were larking about in the altogether because some thief made off with your attire.
Joan } Exactly. { *Speaking*
Angus } { *together*
Sergeant (*complacently*) Where is he then?

Maxie exits

(*Generally*) Where is he then?
Brian Where is he then—*yes*.
Nancy Yes, where *is* he?
Joan Who?
Sergeant This thief of whom you speak so freely.
Joan How should *I* know?
Sergeant Just as I thought. Bang goes your alibi.

Mrs Court-Bending stirs, and comes to

Mrs Court-Bending Officer! Thank Heaven you're here.

The Sergeant executes something midway between a bow and a curtsy

Sergeant Everything under control, sir—thanks to your vigilance.

Mrs Court-Bending gets to her feet and glares at Angus and Joan

Mrs Court-Bending You—*devils.* (*She takes up the case, is about to sweep out, when she suddenly remembers and turns to Eddie*) Oh—Mr Manchip —this is why I came back——

Joan That's *my* case.

Mrs Court-Bending (*ignoring her*) —I seem to have made a terrible mistake. Thought it was all for *me*, you understand. Only realized my mistake when I went through the jolly old pockets. Oh, and there's this. (*She holds up the gun*) You'd better take charge of it, officer.

Mrs Court-Bending hands the gun to the Sergeant, who stares at it. The others start to ravage the suitcase

Nancy That's mine——

Brian —and mine . . .

Mrs Court-Bending As soon as I found all the keys and wallets and things, thought m'self, hello, there's been a jolly old misunderstanding. Oh, and this piece of paper fell out of one of the jackets. Seems to have your signature on it, Mr Manchip . . .

Eddie grabs the I O U from her, stares at it, beams, and rips it into pieces

Eddie You know—whoever you are—*whatever* you are—you've made someone jolly happy. (*He kisses her*)

Mrs Court-Bending (*coyly*) Oh—well—look—*gosh!* I'm most awfully sorry—cheeroh!

Mrs Court-Bending exits through the main doors

Everyone has been grabbing for their clothes, including Brian who passes his pirate-jerkin to Eddie who absent-mindedly puts it on. Brian gets into his own jacket

Eddie (*to the Sergeant*) *Now* do you see what's been going on, Sergeant?

Sergeant Well, sir, it would seem to explain the dearth of raiment currently prevailing in this area. I'd better call off the 'unt.

Mr Butcher staggers in from the Treatment Rooms, sees the Sergeant with the gun and raises his arms above his head

Mr Butcher I can't stand it! What with the 'eat and the law and the local mob—I give in! Take me to a nice cold cell and I'll confess the lot.

Brian There's your man, officer—arrest him!

Sergeant Right! Come along *you*. 'Evening, all.

The Sergeant escorts the wilting Mr Butcher out through the main doors

Brian (*with a sudden thought*) Just a minute—why would he arrest the *butcher*?

Eddie For falsifying a pork chop. I mean, it's simply not kosher.

Nancy (*rounding on Angus*) What were you doing in *that* cupboard—in *that* disguise—you Scotch swine.

Angus (*pointing imperiously*) Go and get dressed, woman!
Nancy (*meekly*) Yes, Angus.

Nancy goes upstairs into her room

Joan (*rounding on Brian*) And as for *you* . . .
Brian (*pointing imperiously*) Go and get dressed, woman! (*He suddenly realises what he has said and winces, waiting for her reply*)
Joan (*meekly*) Yes, darling.

Joan goes upstairs into her room

Angus (*to Brian*) What were you doing here with my wife?
Brian What were *you* doing here with *my* wife?
Eddie There's a perfectly reasonable explanation.
Angus ⎱ Well? ⎰ *Speaking*
Brian ⎰   ⎱ *together*

Eddie opens his mouth, closes it again, before speaking

Eddie Nancy and Brian followed you here.
Angus Followed me? Why?
Eddie Because Nancy knew you were lying about the porridge festival.
Angus All right—it's true—but I came here to do business.
Brian Do you always do business in a broom cupboard with your accountant's wife?
Eddie It's true, Brian. (*He goes and looks pointed at Angus*) Angus came here because, being the good business man he is, he recognizes a gold mine when he sees one. (*He fingers the towel Angus wears. Very pointedly*) Didn't you, Angus?

Angus blusters a second

Angus All right, I'll come clean. I'm here to make you an offer.

Maxie's head appears round the window

Brian You mean you really want to buy this place?
Angus Aye, as a development project. I've the contract here. All we've got to agree on is the price. How much? (*He drops in his sporran and pulls out a document*)

Maxie disappears

Eddie Well—I was thinking of something like twenty thousand . . .
Brian (*moving in*) Well now—speaking not as Edward's brother, but as his business adviser . . .
Angus Aye?
Brian (*deflated*) I've no idea.
Eddie We've had so *many* offers, you see.

Angus You mean someone's been here *before* me?

Brian and Eddie exchange a quick look

Brian ⎱ Yes. ⎰ *Speaking*
Eddie ⎰   ⎱ *together*
Angus Who?

There is a knock at the Staff Rooms door

Brian ⎱
Eddie ⎬ Who's there? ⎰ *Speaking*
Angus ⎰   ⎱ *together*
Maxie (*off*) Harry!

Angus ⎱
Brian ⎬ Harry who? ⎰ *Speaking*
Eddie ⎰   ⎱ *together*
Maxie (*off*) Harry Stottle!
Eddie Harry Stottle! The Greek shipping magnate!

> *Maxie enters from the Staff Rooms. He wears an astrakhan overcoat, a homburg, a huge set of worry-beads, and brandishes a large cigar*

Maxie I take it you have considered my proposition?
Angus My name's McSmith.
Maxie No more argues. (*Looking around*) I like it. I want it. I take it Wrap it up—I put it on my ship.
Angus Twenty thousand!
Eddie Twenty?
Maxie Twenty-five!
Angus Thirty!
Brian Thirty-five!
Maxie Forty!
Angus Forty-five!
Maxie Fifty!
Eddie Fifty-five!
Angus Sixty!
Maxie Sixty-five!
Angus Seventy!
Maxie Seventy-five!
Angus Eighty!
Maxie Eighty-five—ninety—ninety-five—one hundred!
Maxie ⎱
Eddie ⎬ Sold! ⎰ *Speaking*
Brian ⎰   ⎱ *together*
Angus I know when I'm beaten. (*He hands the contract to Maxie and crosses to the Treatment Rooms door*) You're a hard man, Mr Stottle.

Angus exits

Zorba.

Maxie flourishes his pen at the contract

Maxie I make my sign!

Maxie passes the contract to Eddie. Eddie signs it as Brian starts to hum happily, then clap, and then break into a little Greek dance of joy

Brian We've done it—we've done it!

Eddie and Maxie join in the dance until Maxie disengages himself and goes to the main doors

Maxie God bless you, gentlemen—and all who sail in you!

Maxie exits

Brian and Eddie continue dancing

Brian } Good-bye, Maxie! { *Speaking*
Eddie }   { *together*

Brian puts the pirate hat on Eddie; but suddenly they stop dancing with the realization that it was indeed Maxie

Brian } Maxie? { *Speaking*
Eddie }   { *together*

Eddie goes to snatch up the contract

Eddie Worthless!

Brian takes it from him

Brian Not only that—he's signed *my name* to it!

Suddenly Minnie appears from Room 1 at the head of the stairs. She is wearing full wedding regalia and smiles serenely down at them

Minnie Yo-ho-ho! My pirate prince has come for his Minnie—and she is ready for him.

Brian and Eddie stare at her as she descends the stairs like Cinderella at the ball

Eddie Not now, Minnie—please—not *now*.
Minnie I understand. You're worried lest you cannot afford to keep me in the manner to which I would like to become accustomed. But fear not, oh denizen of the deep. I have my dowry.

Eddie } Dowry? { *Speaking*
Brian }   { *together*

Minnie My Post Office Savings Book and the legacy from my auntie.
Eddie (*avarice dawning fast*) How much have you got, Minnie?
Minnie Fifty thousand four hundred and thirty-two pounds, and one new penny.

Eddie ⎱ Fifty thousand four hundred and thirty-two ⎰ *Speaking*
Brian ⎰   pounds——   ⎱ *together*
Minnie —and one new penny.
Eddie And one new penny.

Minnie gazes longingly at him. Brian crosses and puts a brotherly hand on Eddie's shoulder

Brian Edward—you know what you must do, don't you?

Slowly Eddie nods. Brian crosses to ring the desk bell. Then returns to link Eddie's hand to Minnie's

Everyone comes out of their various rooms

Listen, everyone—Edward and Minnie have something wonderful to tell you . . .

Maxie enters from the main doors, beaming, dressed as a vicar and holding a Bible as—

the CURTAIN *falls*

The CURTAIN *rises again quickly to reveal Eddie making a break of it out of the main doors. All the others pursue him, including Mr Butcher, who staggers on from the Staff Rooms, pursued by the Sergeant minus his trousers, pursued by Mrs Court-Bending who brandishes the trousers, as—*

the CURTAIN *falls*

FURNITURE AND PROPERTY LIST

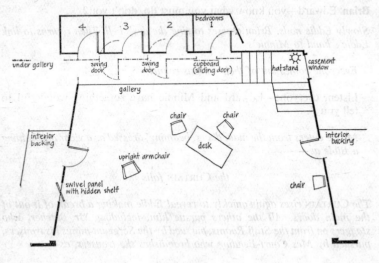

ACT I

SCENE 1

On stage: Desk. *On it:* service bell, telephone, jug of water, writing materials
3 small chairs
1 upright armchair
Hatstand (on landing) *On it:* 2 men's hats
3 antiquated radiators
On walls: wall telephone, posters—one concealing drinks behind swivelling board
In cupboard under stairs: wheelchair with sorbo dummy; blankets; suitcase containing hammer, stethoscope, bottle of horse embrocation, paperback book, large pair of scissors
Carpet
Stair and landing carpets

Off stage: Bottle of vodka (**Eddie**)
I O U (**Mr Butcher**)
Feather duster, bottle of aspirins (**Minnie**)
Brochure (**Mrs Court-Bending**)
Vanity case (**Nancy**)
Suitcase identical to Minnie's, containing clothing (**Joan**)
Steel tape measure (**Minnie**)

                    2 tennis racquets (**Nancy**)
Personal:
                    Eddie: pair of panties wrapped round playing cards
                    Brian: watch
                    Eddie: watch
                    Mrs Court-Bending: watch
                    Minnie: pens and pencils

SCENE 2

Off stage: Bottle of pills (**Maxie**)
              Trunk (**Minnie**)
              Framed oil painting (**Brian**)
              Tennis ball (**Nancy**)
              Sack of tools (**Maxie**)
              Large spanner (**Minnie**)
              Railway lamp, whistle and flag (**Maxie**)
              Lassoo (**Maxie**)
              Stethoscope (**Maxie**)
              Ear trumpet (**Brian**)
              Toga (**Nancy**)

Personal: **Sergeant:** notebook, pencil

ACT II

Off stage: Damp towel (**Joan**)
              Pile of blankets (**Minnie**)
              Pile of Nancy's clothing (**Brian**)
              Large safety pin (**Maxie**)
              Shoulder holster and gun (**Mr Butcher**)
              Telephone (**Brian**)
              Briefcase (**Angus**)
              Violin and bow (**Maxie**)
              Motor-cycle goggles and rubber gloves (**Minnie**)
              Stethoscopes and other medical equipment (**Minnie**)
              Torch (**Maxie**)
              Small hammer (**Maxie**)
              Pile of towels (**Minnie**)
              Bucket with ladles and spoons (**Minnie**)
              Suitcase (Joan's) with toys (**Mrs Court-Bending**)
              Marks & Spencer paper bag (**Brian**)
              Mud-pack (**Nancy**)
              Glass of water (**Maxie**)
              Stuffed parrot (**Maxie**)
              Cutlass, sink plunger for wooden leg (**Brian**)
              Broomstick (**Brian**)
              Hand squeaker (**Sergeant**)
              Contract (**Angus**)
              Set of worry-beads, cigar (**Maxie**)
              Bible (**Maxie**)

LIGHTING PLOT

Property fittings required: nil
Interior. A hall. The same scene throughout

ACT I, SCENE 1. Afternoon

To open: Effect of late autumn sunshine

Cue 1   **Nancy: "Anyone for tennis?"**   (Page 19)
           Black-Out

ACT I, SCENE 2

To open: As Scene 1
No cues

ACT II

To open: As Act I
No cues

EFFECTS PLOT

ACT I

SCENE 1

Cue 1   **Eddie:** "Tell me *what*?"   (Page 4)
Car horn sounds

Cue 2   **Eddie** exits   (Page 11)
Car horn sounds

SCENE 2

No cues

ACT II

Cue 3   As CURTAIN rises   (Page 43)
Sound of police whistles

Cue 4   **Mr Butcher** exits to Treatment Rooms   (Page 48)
Telephone rings

Cue 5   **Nancy:** "How about a tango?"   (Page 55)
Burst of gypsy music: continue to end of dance

Cue 6   **Minnie** enters with dummy   (Page 67)
Sound of police whistles